Write Where You Are

Testimonials

"The best books work on several levels; this short yet powerful and deep tome delivers its message both wide and deep. It reads more like a conversation between the writer and the reader. You feel like you are in the same room as Junie in a workshop. You are gently encouraged to pick up your pen and download the thought streams flowing through your brain onto paper. And most importantly, you are guided to see the meaning and purpose of your writing. The pen is mightier than the sword, and the brevity of this guide belies its power. Pick up this book and write yours."

Tom Evans, author of *Soulwaves: A Future History*

"This work gets to the core purpose of writing, the messaging of the inner soul, and the healing of the heart. "With care, it holds you in its folds and caresses you while you speak your pain, your poetry, your love, and your truth." This book is a delightful, haphazard journey through the purpose of writing with constructive rambling and amusing but poignant anecdotes that urge the reader to put down the book, just for a few moments, and dig out the pen.

Write Where You Are highlights another reason for writing—to heal the soul and use the healing process to help others heal themselves and is filled with words you want to save in your quote bag to share with others. This is not only a book about good writing—it is a book about good living."

Lawrence J. W, Cooper B.A, B Ed., M.Ed.,
author of *Bi: A Bisexual Man's Transformational Journey from Agony to Ecstasy*

"I truly did not believe it could be this easy! Junie, you have no idea how long I have been blocked. Thank you for bringing the writer in me back to life."

Sheila White, *workshop participant*

"Dear Junie, thank you for creating such a sacred, safe, and healing place as this group. I so appreciate the wonderfully spiritual, non-judgmental, supportive, loving, and talented person and facilitator you are. Your deep love of the written word is always evident. During these past weeks, you've given me a deeper appreciation of the benefits and value of this medium, both personally and professionally. I loved the different exercises and processes you offered us. They managed to shake things up inside me and challenged me to stretch myself beyond my comfort zone to a place where I feel confident to do this on my own. Yes, my wisdom lies inside of me, and the writing brings it out in miraculous ways. Finally, thank you for your ever-present humour and sense of fun!"

Irene Boehn-Hill, *workshop participant*

"Dear Junie, when I put pen to paper in the form which you taught me, my heart comes alive and stirs my soul into a recognition and familiarity I've never felt before. You have guided me through my frightened blur of confusion to a place of greater clarity and peace—given each of us a greater understanding of our worth, a reaffirmation that we can do it—and it's worth the effort to get to the other side. Always, your approach is gentle, your manner is intensely present, and your suggestions are appropriate and always heartfelt. Thank you."

Catherine Frieberg-Valaderes, *workshop participant*

"Thank you so much for writing this book! I haven't written for a very long time. Recently I lost my brother and now my mother! The wisdom in *Write Where You Are* has inspired me to put pen to paper again and is helping me move through my deep grief."

Sarah L. *workshop participant*

"I never realized that writing could be that simple. I thought it was a lofty craft accessible only to creatives which I don't consider myself to be. You have made it easy with your writing prompts and exercises, and I am actually finding the words flowing forth now. Thank you, Junie."

Peter W. *workshop participant*

"I love the part in the book where you describe how writing where you are in any given moment can free you. I tried it. I stopped judging where I was in my life—thinking I should be further ahead of where I am...and I also stopped judging what I was writing and just wrote the truth. I couldn't believe how much freer I felt. My problems don't feel as heavy. I can even see some solutions."

Lisa S. *workshop participant*

WRITE WHERE YOU ARE

A Guided Experience for
Those Who Dream of Writing
But Don't Know Where to Begin

JUNIE SWADRON

NEW YORK

LONDON • NASHVILLE • MELBOURNE • VANCOUVER

WRITE WHERE YOU ARE

*A Guided Experience for Those Who Dream of Writing
but Don't Know Where to Begin*

Published in New York, New York, by Morgan James Publishing. Morgan James is a trademark of Morgan James, LLC. www.MorganJamesPublishing.com

Proudly distributed by Publishers Group West®

ISBN 9781636981581 paperback
ISBN 9781636981598 ebook
Library of Congress Control Number:
2023933321

Cover Design by:
Rachel Lopez
www.r2cdesign.com

Interior Design by:
Chris Treccani
www.3dogcreative.net

Morgan James is a proud partner of Habitat for Humanity Peninsula and Greater Williamsburg. Partners in building since 2006.

Get involved today! Visit: www.morgan-james-publishing.com/giving-back

Dedication

I dedicate this book to you, my readers. My deepest wish is that if your soul guides you to write, you will be open to its sacred offerings and learn the satisfaction of wordplay on the page that can heal your heart or invoke your muse as nothing else can. You will have found a loyal friend forever when writing becomes that for you.

I thank the thousands of writing students I have had the privilege of coaching for close to three decades. Because of you, I show up year after year with the same passion as I did when I presented my very first writing workshop in 1994, called *Write Where You Are*.

Finally, I thank my little red diary with its lock and key, which, at only eleven years old, opened the writer in me and put me on a majestic path I could not have ever imagined. Writing became my sacred practice, a meditation on the page. Every time I sit down to write, God sits beside me, whispering the words that I need to hear.

Contents

Acknowledgments

Without a moment's hesitation, I humbly thank my friend and colleague, Nan Campbell, who read and guided me through the pages of this latest edition. It is because of her expertise as a writer, author, and former *Write Where You Are* student that I am overjoyed and confident that this book will deliver everything in my heart that I hoped it would.

Thank you to Morgan James for seeing the value of this book, wanting it to be in as many hands as possible—for people who wish to write but are not sure where and how to begin—and therefore agreed wholeheartedly to take it on.

I thank Megan McConnell, my proofreader and editor, for making sure all the i's are dotted and t's are crossed, and for her excellent eye for detail and outstanding suggestions that made the final manuscript one I am delighted to bring forth into the world.

Thank you to my countless writers over three decades who have graced me with your presence. Thank you for your willingness to be vulnerable and try to write even when you were scared or embarrassed. In short, thank you for trusting me with the process and for rewarding me with your successes each and every time!

And lastly, thank you to *you*, dear reader, whom I know, as you pick up your pen and *write where you are*, you will find a treasure-trove of stories, insights, creativity, and wisdom accompanying you on your writing journey.

Write-fully yours,

Junie

Foreword

Junie Swadron's new edition is a small, personal treasure to all who seek a combination of self-knowledge, inner peace, and direct access to fluid, authentic, verbal self-expression. She is also a community builder who brings people together in writing circles, where active listening without judgment and sharing without self-censoring or deprecation is the guiding ethic.

For decades, Junie has been actively mentoring individuals and groups in this process, which has led her to find her own means of life-sustaining self-expression. She has coaxed and coached numerous people into finding their groove with her writing tools. She has midwifed many a fumbling, insecure beginning into finding its birth as a book. She has a big heart that sings at each person's baby steps and strides.

Junie is not someone you put on a pedestal as a "writer" or "mentor," though she clearly is both to workshop participants and individual writing students alike. Junie presents herself honestly and openly wherever she is in her own process at any given moment. In this way, she models how the courage of vulnerability can be coupled with the commitment to keep on storytelling one's truth. In this way, rather than an "expert," which she clearly is, she presents herself as gently there, beside you: a fellow traveller who is just a bit ahead of you on the path. Junie's intimate humanity invites her readers to lower those inhibiting barriers of fear, judgment, and crippling comparisons and just get on with it—yep, the writing. And when you are stuck or lost, she has just the right tool up her sleeve to get you moving and found again.

I have had the privilege of taking several larger workshops with Junie and of joining her at her Sunday writing circles in her home. In her workshop gatherings, she creates a sharing community around her and even evokes a sense of communion.

This book is wonderfully interactive in an old-fashioned way, with no electricity or electronics needed. Sharing story-telling glimpses of her own journey, Junie Swadron also offers many creative, concrete writing exercises and practical tips for how to navigate around and past any roadblocks that appear between living small and accessing your fullness in creative, courageous living. And your writing will sing in whatever genre you play in and publish (or not).

Astri Wright, Ph.D. Writer; Artist; Professor of Art History, University of Victoria, BC, Canada.

Introduction

Journal entry: 7:45 a.m.

"It's the 22nd of January. It's raining outside. The snow melted yesterday, and the streets became a sheet of ice. The first phone call I received this morning came from Jeannette, telling me, "I don't know if I can make the writing group today because the entire street is a skating rink, and I'm afraid to drive."

Wendy called next, "Did you hear about the highways last night? Listen, I know you have a writing group soon, but I just thought I'd tell you the streets are crazy. Call me later."

The phone rang again. Joe.

"Hi, Joe," I muttered. "Yes, I know; the streets are a sheet of ice, and you're not coming."

"How did you know what I was going to say?" He sounded surprised.

"Because I've been getting a constant stream of weather reports."

"Well, I'm going to try and make it. I have my trusty umbrella, woollen earmuffs, gloves, and galoshes. Hope to see you, but you know what it's like around here. Could turn into a blizzard. Bye."

When the phone rings again, anxiety penetrates my whole body. Maybe I won't answer it. Not another call about the weather and who's not coming.

Then I remember to breathe. I remember my Zen teachings. Be in the moment. Unattached. It's all okay. I breathe again. And then it gets better."

So, that journal entry was from many years ago, and I admit, I wasn't as evolved then. I wouldn't say I'm enlightened now either, but at least I wouldn't be telling my students, "A blizzard? Big deal. Risk your life. Writing is all that matters." Well, I wasn't actually saying that. Was I?

From our point of view, for the duration of the pages of this book, writing IS all that matters. So, get your rain gear, snow gear, and sun gear, go to the nearest café, beach, bench, or kitchen table and get out your writing gear!

Okay, back to my journal pages from all those years ago...

"It's 9:45, and the buzzer starts ringing, and the people start coming, and the hum of the energy in the room is magical, and before I know it, we're all writing, we're all connecting, and the beauty and comfort unfolds."

True. That's what happens in a sacred circle. A sacred circle is created through safety. It is not a critique group, as many writing groups tend to be, but rather a sacred place where everyone is held in the highest esteem. There is an acceptance. It provides a place where even the most hesitant person can read what they've written and learn how it feels to be fully supported wherever they are.

And through this process, their voice gets stronger, and one day, they notice that their voice on the page has become their voice in the world. Not necessarily in published works, but in the way they stand taller, in the way they feel more confident and know their mind, and in the way that their inner child who still lives within them knows that she or he matters.

The purpose of this book is to enhance the qualities that happen in a sacred writing circle within your heart. A breathing space that holds and caresses you when you feel weary or delights you when you feel whimsical and dreamy. A place to take off your shoes, remove the societal masks, and show up just as you are.

Now, pour yourself a cup of tea or coffee, or whatever happens to be your tipple of choice, as I invite you to come home to yourself in the pages of your journal.

Love,

Junie

Part One
WRITE YOURSELF HOME

Rekindling Wholeness and Peace on the Page

What does it mean to "write yourself home?" For me, it's an expression of writing that originates from deep within your heart and spirit. Your soul awaits you here. You only need to step to the side and let the words flow forth. There's a kindness here, a beckoning, a sense of wholeness.

In recognizing that writing is a sacred art, you learn about self-acceptance, honouring and letting go of self-judgments about how you write. It's a place of honouring yourself, the child that lives within you, and the journey upon which you are about to embark.

This book can be used as a lantern to shed light on the deepest portal of your subconscious mind. From this place of original thoughts, feelings, and images, words are birthed onto the page. You are simply tapping into what is already there and writing it down.

What is it, why is it, and how is it that when you write where you are in the moment—it could be about any subject under the sun—and then share it with someone who is not judging you, you feel lighter, calmer, more present, and somehow, more healed?

My students constantly tell me, "I didn't even know that I felt this way; it just came out in the writing."

"How do you feel?" I ask. "Like a unified choir," they reply, "Better. I feel better."

Sometimes, I think it's too simple. But then I realize that's exactly why it's so powerful. Because it's that simple. Writing from where we are, in this very moment, is a process of truth-telling. You may be flooded with emotion while you impart how you feel onto the pages. Feelings such as:

Sadness or grief: perhaps, someone dear to you died recently or left town, and you miss them beyond measure.

Outrage: you discover your pearl necklace has gone missing. Your teenage daughter confesses that she "borrowed" it. Then she tells you that she accidentally left it in Italy when she was there last month with your estranged ex and his new girlfriend. You live in Texas. You want to strangle her.

Excitement: your lover just called and said he bought tickets for a night at the opera. You adore opera. Immediately, you fantasize about what you will wear.

Undefined emotions: a guy you knew a million years ago found you on Facebook and wants to "catch up with you." You swore you would never give him the time of day after he suddenly left you without a goodbye. You married Thomas right afterward, and only you know that your heart never healed. What do you do?

This is where your journal can show off its magic. If you write through the process of allowing, not trying to dictate the outcome, your answers will become clear.

Does this happen every time? Not necessarily. But for me, something always shifts when I write it down.

So, if it's whirling around inside your head, write where you are. Don't embellish or deny; just say it as it is. Of course, you can make it up as you go along, which is what creative license is all about. However, when it comes to real emotion, it is best to name it how you feel it. Why keep disturbing thoughts and feelings sifting around in your stomach? Instead, why not drop them onto the page to be honoured or, conversely, crunched up and tossed into the garbage pail instead of causing a stomach ache and, over time, an ulcer?

Just write and see where it takes you. Then move on. Moving on could be wearing your sexy red chiffon dress to the opera, grounding your daughter for a year, or meeting that beau from thirty years ago only to have your original suspicions confirmed—he is still charming, convincing, and dangerous.

You leave room for clarity when you release what you genuinely feel onto the page without judging, exaggerating, or editing. Also, in time, and sometimes even as you put down your pen, you will have a sense of spaciousness that wasn't there before.

This is akin to free-flow, stream-of-conscious journal writing, the essence of this book. And, once you grasp the process, which is easy as pie—if you like pie—you can then apply it to whatever you choose to write. Fiction, non-fiction, poetry, blogs, business reports, academic papers, etc.

"Excuse me?" You may ask. "Free-flow, stream-of-conscious writing in business reports and academic papers? Get real!"

Absolutely!

Give it a fresh, personal, creative approach so that the reader doesn't get bored to tears. Nor the writer, for that matter.

So, what makes me a self-proclaimed authority?

Especially when my shrink asked suspiciously, "You what? You want to facilitate writing groups? Do you have credentials? Wouldn't that take a lot of chutzpah?"

As soon as those words left his lips, my faint heart fell onto the cold, lonesome ground, only to get buried there and trampled on for eternity. I saw people gathering around the mound, placing their prayers and flowers upon it while he enlightened them with his poetry.

Luckily, he took me out of that trance with his next words, "Junie," he declared with conviction. "I say, go for it!"

Oh, he was a jokester, all right. But not very funny. One more minute and I would have needed resuscitation.

Anyhow, luckily, my over-stimulated imagination got re-directed to a brighter purpose, and I did go for it. And I've been a writing coach ever since.

Back to *Write Where You Are*. Why did I name my classes and this book, *Write Where You Are?*

Well, for sure, it's a cutsie phrase. Hmm, how do you spell "cutsie?" I'm getting a red line under the word on my computer.

Wait, I'll click spell-check. Darn. It only shows the words: cutie, cutesier—whatever that is—and curtsied. Okay, I'll check the thesaurus. Geez, it says, "No results found." After all that, it's not even a word! Now I'm frustrated.

I bet you're wondering why I'm verbalizing my frustration about not finding the right spelling or even that the word exists. Well, since I'm convinced that you are asking that question, I'm happy to give you the answer. It's because I just committed the first "no-no" rule in free-flow, stream-of-conscious, let-it-rip writing—which you can tell this is!

The number one cause for throwing in the towel for would-be writers is that they stop themselves outright. Sometimes, in the very first paragraph. They'll stop by the end of the first line if they are true perfectionists. Which I just illustrated. Not a reflection of myself, of course. Just mentioning it for teaching purposes.

Ahem. Okay. Busted.

Well, I'm not the only one. You're busted, too if you say the following is foreign to you. You write something and then say to yourself, "Hmm, this doesn't look right—I'd better check the spelling. Maybe I should use a different word, more sophisticated, perhaps? Oh, and I can't believe I was about to write that. Thank goodness I stopped myself. What if I die before dinner, and my journal's sitting on the coffee table? They'll think I've written my suicide note. If I were alive, I'd be mortified."

Am I close?

If this seems even vaguely familiar, this is where editing as you write, which is an absolute no-no, will make your ego throw a party. "Screw this," it'll say. "I'm out of here." So, you burn your journal and go dancing. My recommendation would be to scribble all that down first and then go dancing. Oh, and hide your journal under your mattress before you go. I can't imagine anyone would ever think to look there. Wink, wink, nod, nod.

But what if it's true? You really are fed up with what does or doesn't come out of your pen, and you want to ditch the writing, check your emails, go to the mall, eat a chocolate bar, or catch the next flight to Vegas to gamble away your savings?

I can tell you, with confidence, that there are probably as many reasons, which are usually really excuses, to stop writing as there are "blocked" writers. So, what's the antidote?

Simple. Write.

Does this surprise you? Of course not. You knew I was going to say that, right? Write. That's the only thing that will move you beyond your excuses. When you want to lose weight, you stay away from the fridge. When you want to learn skydiving, you show up at the hangar. When you want to write, you keep your pen on the page or keyboard and your hand moving.

While in the creative process, which is every time you sit down at your writing table, except when you deliberately go there to edit, you let it have its way with you. That means that you don't give a hoot about how the word is spelled. Or whether it fits in that particular paragraph or the next one down. Or whether so and so will like it. Or whether it would be better to use a semi-colon instead of a period.

Do hide it, though. And maybe in a better place than under the mattress.

That's about it. You're ready to write. Don't panic, we'll start slowly. Here are the instructions. Grab a pen. Set your timer for five minutes. No cheating—five minutes—Eezy Peezy.

And NO editing as you go.

WRITING PROMPT: Today, the sun is shining, and my dog went for a walk without me.

Now, it could be a blazing blizzard outside where you are, which would definitely cause concern for your dog. Or it is 2 a.m., and you can't sleep, which is why you're here with your pen and paper ready. And it doesn't matter if you don't have a dog. In this exercise, you begin your piece with, *The sun is shining, and my dog went for a walk without me.* Okay, timer set? Don't stop before it goes off. And you must promise not to look ahead. I'll write too. Go!

_____

_____

_____

_____

_____

_____

_____

_____

_____

_____

_____

_____

_____

_____

_____

_____

_____

_____

_____

_____

Buzz. Ding Dong. Psst. Time's up. Put down that pen.

I can't believe I said that. Ignore me—keep writing if you're on a roll.

Here's what I wrote:

The sun is shining, and my dog went for a walk without me. I could have sworn I was holding onto the leash with Munchkin on the end of it while talking to Sally Graves who brings the mail. We meet up the same time every day, 11:11 a.m. it's just right for Munchkin and me. He's already programmed in the time and doesn't even wait till she's at the door, I swear He senses her at the end of the block coming this way and he's at the door barking and wagging his tail. Sally Graves starts telling me that she and her new guy are moving in together and are looking for new place.

He complained about how crowded he felt in her messy place, and she complained about how she goes nuts in his pristine living quarters where she's afraid to eat in case a crumb drops on the floor (but are apparently compatible in every other way) they are searching out new digs but in Africa where she lived as a kid. It was on his bucket…

TIME. Five minutes are up.

How did you do?

Don't say that you didn't do it.

And, if you didn't, then go back and do it. Until then, you cannot pass go and cannot collect $200.00 or 200 pounds, rupees, shekels, or pesos, or have dessert before dinner.

If you did write for the last five minutes, then congratulations. Say to yourself, "I did it!"

Now, get up and do the happy dance. I'm serious. Because, if you're not accustomed to writing—and there's a good chance that that's why you're reading this amazing book—then the thing is, you wrote, and that's fantastic. Seriously.

However, if you said to yourself, "Yeah, I wrote, but it sucks." that doesn't count. I will have to relegate you to the back of the class, where I've installed my fool-proof "I Love Myself" simulator machine. Once you step inside, you immediately get fast-tracked through my signature programme in radical self-loving. You will step out ten timeless minutes later, egoless, without a trace of fear or self-doubt left. Only love and confidence remain.

Not bad hug? Oops, I meant to say, "huh." Come here; let me give you a hug before you go.

Back to writing. The rule is, even though I said there are none, there's this one: Absolutely no judging the writing in your journal. None. Full stop. Non-negotiable. End of story.

Take my five-minute writing piece, for example. You may have noticed that it has a whole bunch of run-on sentences, a slew of missing commas or periods and spelling mistakes. I never found out where Munchkin went or whether I ever saw him again. Or Sally Graves, for that matter, since she was taking off with her new guy. To Africa.

And that's how it works; you just write. It's not about good, bad, right, or wrong. It's just the way it is. That's what makes journal writing so enchanting.

And the same goes for any kind of writing that calls for imagination and unlimited wordplay or simply telling your truth. Instead of a critical mind, akin to bumper cars crashing into each other at the country fair, leaving you battered and bruised, you get to rest your heart on the page with your words without any concern for how they show up.

Now, back to why I call my classes, *Write Where You Are*. This is more than a play on words, which could be considered cutsie—however you spell it—but the truth is, it's all about being in the moment, which we've all heard plenty about. You cannot live in this era and not have heard or hopefully experienced mindfulness and the power of being in the moment.

It's the same for writing. When you write where you are in this present moment, your energy comes alive. And the words that free-fall onto the page are ecstatic because they're being liberated. This holds true even when you write about something that happened twenty years ago because your relationship to it now matters. And your writing will show you what matters even when you yourself are not sure. Why? Because the truth always comes to the surface when you ask your ego to step to the side.

Ahh, that disgusting ego again! That awful part of you is addicted to being right rather than happy and insists on making you sweat the small stuff. How's that for a bunch of clichés?

Writing Tip

If you come back to your journals to extract passages to edit for other purposes, try to find metaphors rather than clichés. Just sayin'.

Back to the ego. At some point, it's wise to befriend this evil gremlin, but for now, let's just send the monster to a 12-Step Program for letting go of control. Or have love and compassion for him, her, it. That's another lesson, though. And a stretch.

If you truly want to learn how you can book a therapy appointment with me. Or, much advised and cheaper, take out your journal and write your thoughts about it. You'll find your answers on the page. I only pretend to have them for you. And then charge you for it. Good gig, huh?

Anyway, here's what Natalie Goldberg says about the little beasties in her famous book, *Writing Down the Bones*, which is worth buying, in my opinion, and cheaper than hiring me. Tell her I said that, and maybe I'll get a commission. Ya think?

In her chapter "Trouble with the Editor," Natalie Goldberg talks about how important it is to separate you as the creator from you as the editor or internal critic when you're writing. This way, your creator has the freedom to breathe, explore and express. She goes on to say that if you're having difficulty distinguishing between your creative voice and the annoying voice of your internal editor, take some time to let your editor have its full voice. In other words, write down all your internal critiques, and get the words on the page so you can fully release the energy around them.

Sound familiar?

Goldberg says that the more clearly you know your inner editor, the better you can ignore it. After a while, it becomes noise in the background. She advises that you don't reinforce its power by listening to its empty words. So, if your inner critic says your writing is boring and you listen to it and stop writing, that reinforces and gives credence to your editor. Your inner editor knows exactly which words will stop you from writing! Let the words roll off your back and keep writing, no matter what your inner critic or editor says. You could even answer with, "So what if my writing is boring? So what!"

This book is all about that. The one you're holding in your hands or reading on a screen. It will help you use writing as a tool to express both your creativity and heal your heart. When you don't judge what you write, you will be set free, which is akin to healing your heart.

The practices in *Write Where You Are* will teach you how to use writing as a self-awareness tool to foster understanding, reduce stress, and access insight and wisdom. And it's to show you a safe place to go with things you may not know how to express otherwise. It will help you move blocked energy and breathe gently into new beginnings as you discover who you are, helping you to make sense of your life and giving you direction, purpose, and clarity.

From this, you will see unlimited uses for your journal and unlimited results. Become open to the possibility that your entries will astound you, where your deepest grief becomes a story filled with pain and courage that helps to heal your heartbreak or a poem that you send to a love interest that opens his heart to love you back, and he arrives at your door and proposes, and you move to his sailboat and cross the seas to romantic vistas and live happily ever after. Sorry, I got caught up in my own daydream. What Evverr! You get the point!

Consider yourself a storyteller of the events in your life. Look at each with the eyes of a curious child instead of the eyes of a critic. When you do, you will discover that your journal has become your very best friend.

Your mother, partner, counsellor, and best mate are not always available when you want them, but your journal will be. Patiently, it waits for you to feed it and doesn't tell you it's starving because you haven't fed it in months.

Nor does it tell you it's suffocating in the drawer that you stuffed it in or buried under a dozen books on the table. No, it is completely loyal. You may desert it, but it will never leave you. You can tell it about the same things over and over again, and it will never say in all sarcasm, "You've already said that a thousand times. Get over it already!" You can rage onto its pages, and it will remain equally non-judgmental. Well, it may cry out in terror, "Please, don't rip me up or set me on fire!"

That's not even funny! I don't know who wrote that. It wasn't me. I would never. Honestly. It must be an evil entity that took over my hand on the keys just now.

Another thing that Natalie Goldberg says is that you should keep your hand moving and write quickly, so that mean ego gremlin—in this case, a nasty entity—can't catch up to you and say evil things.

Okay, the real truth—and I know about these things—is that your journal is like your guardian angel. With care, it holds you in its folds and caresses you while you speak your pain, poetry, love, and truth.

I was fortunate enough to discover the benefits of a diary when I was a young girl, long before the term journaling became part of the popular vernacular.

My mother never said, "Junie, go to your room and write in your journal; it will make you feel better." But luckily, I found it out on my own anyway, and it became my safe haven in a world that often didn't feel safe. That little red diary, with its tiny lock and key, became my refuge, my private sanctuary, and a place to hide out yet not feel alone. Within its pages, words just flowed from my heart, becoming a meditation on the page, often restoring me to sanity. Over the years, it has become my lifeline. My loveline. My way out of the wilderness.

I would open a page, and it felt as if a benevolent presence sat with me while I emptied whatever I felt onto the blank sheets. In time, I came to believe that a sacred, unseen companion waited patiently to guide my hand and help me heal my soul.

Will writing a journal do this for you? I don't know. There is, however, an excellent chance of it, along with a whole bunch of other good stuff, and you won't know until you make space for it in your life.

I believe that each of you needs a private place where you can express yourself without censorship or judgment or someone telling you it's wrong, impolite, unforgiving, or something else. Each of you needs somewhere to unburden yourself on your own and know it's completely safe to do so. Also, it's so important simply to have a welcoming friend, no matter what state you're in.

My objective for writing this book is to show you what I discovered so long ago; how your diary, your journal, or whatever name you wish to give it, can be your best buddy for life.

And you will find that free-style journal writing often spills into creative writing in every genre.

Julia Cameron's "Morning Pages" were fodder for her famous book, *The Artist's Way.* You never know where your Muse could be hiding. After wrestling for weeks in my journal, anguished from yet another hospitalization for depression—part of a revolving door caused by bipolar disorder—soul messages from my pen implored me to tell my story, which one year later birthed my play, *Madness, Masks, & Miracles.*

And I can tell you, when the messages came through, I was too busy writing them to worry about them being grammatically correct. How refreshing it is to toss out the old rule books. No one cares if you can't spell cutsie!

It won't matter where you start your sentences or where you finish off. And it doesn't matter if you doodle in between paragraphs. It doesn't matter how you do it. You can't make a mistake. You can only get it right when there is no wrong or right.

Yet don't feel surprised that even after I tell you this, you will still want to do this perfectly. It's just what we creatures of habit do.

Here's the scenario: you're going to take out your journal and first wonder if it's the right size. "Perhaps, I should have bought a smaller one and one without lines so that I can draw when I don't want to write." You'll begin to write and will wonder if you should have started there. You'll forge on, and your mind will want to go somewhere else. You'll fight with it to stay on topic, but it'll become laborious, so you'll throw your hands up in the air and shout, "Whose idea was this, anyway? Everyone says it's so easy, but it's not working for me! I knew it. I might as well give it up." And then you will. And you'll leave frustrated and unfulfilled and wonder what all the hype about writing is about. Next, you'll grab your jacket and go golfing.

How do I know this to be true more often than not? Because I've been a writing coach for approximately three decades, and the biggest common denominator that holds would-be writers back is the lack of confidence, which I see over and over again.

Unfortunately, it's far more natural to criticize than compliment yourself. It's easier to quit than keep on going and seeing what unfolds. So, if you find yourself doing this, even after I tell you that there are no rules, don't get discouraged. I am sending you back to that trusty "I Love Myself" simulating machine. You will come out writing and not giving a hoot about what's travelling out of your pen. You'll be too busy writing.

The key is that you stop being attached to any outcome. And that's when it becomes fun, which is totally worth waiting for. That's when it becomes a way of life. You sit down to write, and you write. It's just a journal. It's for your eyes only. It's not going to be juried for the Booker Award. It's your journal, and writing in it can be your key to freedom. Just like anything. At first, it takes practice. Then it's like getting up and brushing your teeth—you don't think about how to do it; you already know how.

And, when writing becomes that for you, you'll notice a shift in your life. You will see that things are working out better. You will observe that your voice on the page has become stronger. Even if, a few days later, you change your mind about what you said, and a new truth emerges, that's okay. In fact, it's what happens when we write from our authentic voice. We move the energy around instead of staying stuck in it. We find a healthier, newer way to relate to the situation. Clarity emerges. New life energy emerges. Strength, confidence, and self-love show up. As you continue to write, don't let it surprise you when you achieve things that you never thought possible.

If you're an adult reading this, hold your hand on your heart and say to your little child in there, "It's safe to come out, honey. Even though stupid Miss So-and-So in Grade 6 scratched red lines through your beautiful compositions, I won't let that happen ever again. I'm not going to criticize and judge you. I'm not going to tell you that you can't write. You can write whatever, and however you like. I am here to embrace you, love you, be kind to you, and give you back the voice you never had. I love you, my beautiful little child, and I want you to help teach me everything I've forgotten."

After I had abandoned her for most of my life, I hungered for my little girl inside to trust me. I took on a ridiculous never-ending to-do list and trampled the creativity right out of her. I still have a huge to-do list, but I also take time to listen to her needs more than I used to.

She knows that she can say whatever she wants. On the page, I let her have her way with me, and when I neglect her needs, oh boy, does she ever get mad. I get embarrassed, and we have a truce. I walk down to the beach and let her sing to the mermaids and unicorns to her heart's desire.

This is how the simulator works, to tell you the truth. The more I listen to my heart, my inner child, my still small voice, the voice I rest on the page or build into the echo chambers of my sand castles, then the more faith I have in life. My journal brings my lost parts back home again. My reclaimed voice sets me free.

So, once again, get your rain gear, snow gear, and sun gear, go to the nearest café, beach, bench, or kitchen table and get out your writing gear!

Write and enjoy!

Part Two

WHY PEOPLE HATE TO WRITE AND WOULD RATHER DO ANYTHING ELSE

Believe me, you are not alone if you hate to write and would rather do anything else, including eating bugs for breakfast, staying adrift at sea, or inviting your in-laws—who wish their son or daughter (you decide) had married someone else—to move in with you.

In this section, you may think you have died and gone to heaven because you are not singing solo. You have been cast in an international choir. Dissident, perhaps, but at least you're not alone. Don't go AWOL on me if you recognize yourself in any of the following scenarios. I would never leave you in your discomfort. I have solutions.

You know how you sometimes must swallow the same poison to acquire enough antibodies to fight what you're trying to avoid? However, I'll settle for this one since I couldn't think of a different example. Consider the following solution as the antidote for your disdain for writing. And luckily for you, one size fits all.

Drum roll, please. Ta-da!

Write!

I know, by now, you have caught on to the fact that I'm redundant and predictable. And I'm proud of you for it. And I'm proud of myself, too. Because this is a tried-and-true method, I don't give up easily, even at the risk of being redundant and predictable. In fact, it's not easy being me, trying to convince you how easy writing is when you hate it and would rather be doing anything else. And, if you're beyond that, if what you read in Part One convinced you and you're miles ahead, don't read this section. It could stop you.

However, for those who are continuing, each yucky condition stated below is followed by a writing exercise that allows you to exorcize the feelings that come up right afterward. They're nice exercises, though. I believe that you'll like them. They get right to the point—something I'm not known for! By now, you probably want to tear your hair out or are ready to acquiesce just to get it over with. Humour me. Do the latter. Or are you cursing me, saying, "What does she think? I'm a moron? I hate writing, and her way of solving the situation is to write! Who's the moron here?" Good, you're starting to get it now. Write it down.

Back to the choir you may be singing in.

Shame

One of the most common reasons that some people would rather do anything else than write is because they were shamed in school.

Their essays or short stories got marked up with red pens. They got criticized for poor spelling, told their ideas weren't original, and that they had lots to learn about grammar. And on and on it went.

All they learned was that to write, they had to be perfect.

Imagine a toddler getting ridiculed for not pronouncing his first words correctly. If he said "meema" instead of "momma," would you let him know in so many words that he's an idiot?

I love what Mark Twain had to say about this, that if we teach our children to speak the way we teach them to write, we would all stutter!

That's ludicrous. Yet it happened to many innocent children after they wrote their first composition filled with imagination and handed it in for the teacher to mark. They were shamed for their spelling mistakes and the fact that this sentence should have been followed by that one, and since when are trees aqua-marine?

Shame still plagues many adults from their youth for being told they weren't doing it right. Worse, it turned them into perfectionists. And even if it wasn't about writing, maybe they were criticized when they tried singing, painting or woodworking—writing became just one more thing that they believed they couldn't do.

I've had countless adults tip-toe tentatively into my classes and bring with them all the courage they could muster because that's exactly what happened to them decades earlier. Yes, shame still plagues many adults from their youth for being told they weren't doing it right.

If you have had an experience like that, now is your chance to toss out etiquette and spill your beans. Are you angry? Or have you stuffed it down so long that you feel numb? This is your opportunity to reclaim your voice. This is one of those times when your voice on the page can become your voice out in the world. Perhaps it's a voice you've kept hidden all your life.

Well, it's time to step into the light, in fact, the limelight. You're long past due. First, you must take back your power. You have every right to feel furious. Get your anger onto the page. The same goes for frustration, numbness, or the shame you've carried all these years from someone's ignorant comments.

Write where you are right now. Numb? You can start with, "I don't even feel it anymore. You did such a good job at shaming me, I lost my confidence about most things. Even the thought of writing in a journal no one would read makes me queasy. Thanks, one heck of a lot, you mean friggin' jerk! How dare you! Who were you to do that to me? You wrecked my life!"

Now, you're getting it. You're tossing out politeness. Keep going as you imagine how that child or teenager in you must have felt. Feel compassion for your younger self and let her or him have their day in court. Say it all. Oh, and although it might feel tempting, do not send it to your teacher or anyone else for whom the memories of which might invoke these kinds of feelings in you, assuming he or she remains in the land of the living.

You've had enough repercussions already. However, you can go first-class in your imagination. See him or her sitting in a chair in front of the class, wearing a dunce hat and balancing a pickle on her or his nose. And take it from there.

After you've said it all, go out and do something fun. Take that kid in you to the dollar store and get colour stickers to put in your journal that say, "You aced it, kid!" Or, much better, go skiing to the top of Mt. Everest and declare to the world: "I did it! I finally told her off!" Or go to a karaoke club and sing "My Way" or whatever you fancy at the top of your lungs. Don't worry about keeping the beat. You're dancing to the rhythm of your drum now.

Then, someday, when you're daring to go one step further, and the child inside feels safe, you can write a different scenario. Like this one, perhaps:

Imagine being in front of your teacher now that you have reclaimed your power. You feel centred, calm, confident, and clear. Imagine stating how it felt when she or he did that. How it affected your life. Imagine your teacher listening with his or her heart and telling you they're sorry.

In fact, what's incredibly effective and worth the time is to write a letter back to yourself from your teacher whom you imagine has, indeed, learned a lesson or two, has transformed and evolved and is expressing just that. The wounded child in you couldn't hear it often enough.

However, don't leap too soon into forgiveness. First, let yourself express everything you've felt—give your wounded child his or her full voice.

This is my letter and the response from my teacher as I imagine she would write it:

Miss Simmons, how could you? How could you have ever been a teacher—a teacher to little kids? Did you have any idea what you did to us? Did to me!!!! I hate you for it.

Okay, I've gone beyond it now, but does it make it right? No, I will never condone your horrible, despicable behaviour. Teachers are supposed to model kindness and compassion and hone confidence in the students they teach. Help them with the tough subjects and make them feel okay even if they screw up. Make learning fun! Not you. You bully! You despicable bully. I was only eleven years old! Eleven, for goodness' sake!

Did you have any idea what was happening to me at home? Do you have any idea that school was going to be my escape? School was not just a prison; it was a torture chamber. You hated me, and you made it known every single day! You shamed me again and again in front of my classmates. When my marks were the lowest, and you made that call, you failed me over and over again. You would hand out the papers letting everyone know that I had a D or an E, as an example of what happens when you don't pay attention. You were hideous. And to Larry too. Demanding that both of us stay after school, then hovering over us with a smirk on your face, shouting that we were stupid, that we were a disgrace and that you would fail us! And you did. You did! On the last day of school, I went home with big red FAILED scribbled across my report card. Oh, I can imagine your smug satisfaction when you did that.

You have no idea how you wrecked my life with the shame I carried for decades. How insecure I became. How I wore a million masks to hide the humiliation, believing I was stupid. I was terrified to give my opinion about anything. The only thing that comforted me was my little red diary with its lock and key.

Miss Simmons, you had an opportunity to make life a little easier for me. With kindness. With patience and compassion. With something that would make me not want to run away forever, or still the relentless voices in my head that constantly put me down no matter how hard

I tried. Even later, in university, I was convinced my professors made a mistake whenever I got an A or even a B.

It has been over half a century since you lectured and bullied me. Since I felt sickened every morning when I woke up and had to trudge to school, across the creek to Baycrest Avenue Public School. Many days, I simply stayed at the creek, watching the baby frogs leaping up on the banks and the tadpoles swimming without a care. Oh, I knew I would pay big time for playing hooky, but I couldn't help it. Facing you was so much worse.

Now, over fifty years later, do you have something you want to say to me?

Sincerely,

Junie

Dear Junie, words can't make it better. But if they could, I would tell you how truly sorry I am. If I could do it over, I would take you into my heart and offer you love and compassion.

Of course, I saw your pain. Of course, I saw how frightened you were. And it pleased me to lash out at you. I am so ashamed. I had my own struggles and unhealed pain, and it was my way to take it out on the beautiful children who came to me to educate them, encourage them, and teach them in a way that they would feel good about themselves.

But this isn't about me. It's about you, dearest Junie. I remember you and how horrible I was to you, and I am so very, very sorry. Thank you for coming to me so many years later to call me on what I did to you. I can't take it back.

I am only happy and grateful that you moved on. That somehow, along life's path, you were able to move beyond the horrors of your young life, which I was a big part of, and make a good life for yourself.

Sincerely,

Miss Simmons

Later, after giving myself breathing space to integrate this visceral experience, I wrote a brief letter of forgiveness to close the door on this chapter.

Dear Miss Simmons, I am sorry, too, for whatever happened to you in your life that made you that way. I hope you have forgiven yourself and found peace in your heart.

I forgive you,

Junie

WRITING PROMPT: When _____ did/ or said_____ to me, I felt_____. Today I am ready to express myself fully right here by saying…

_____

_____

_____

_____

_____

_____

_____

_____

_____

_____

_____

_____

_____

_____

_____

_____

_____

_____

_____

_____

_____

_____

_____

_____

_____

_____

_____

Afraid of Thoughts and Feelings and Just Wanting to be Nice

Everyone judges. Even on the page. Admittedly, me too. But if you dare tell anyone that, I'll judge you for it! We judge other people, and we judge ourselves.

Mostly, our judgments originate from the people who shamed us in the first place, and we end up thinking that we can never do anything write. Oops, I meant "right." See! I could go to town on that one if I let myself. I could imagine you laughing at me, "Looky here. She's the writing teacher and just screwed up." But luckily, I refuse to take that road to town unless it's to buy a new dress. Taffeta. Retro.

I spent most of my life putting myself down and couldn't help projecting those putdowns onto others. Until, eventually, I stopped. How did I do it? With lots of therapy. And lots of journaling.

Your journals provide the safest place to judge, complain, and state everyone's faults—starting with your own. Yup, you can judge until you have nothing to judge anymore because, despite yourself telling it like it is unwittingly helped you heal your wounds. One day, you noticed that you simply weren't complaining. If you find your life too boring, you can fake it now and again for old times' sake. On the page.

In the meantime, if that's not where you are, don't worry; your journal is singing, "Bring it on! I've got a strong spine!"

Try to suspend judgment (that word again) and write anyway. And when you do, I caution you not to cover up your less-than-loving opinions with flowery words to make them sound pretty and poetic because you want to be nice.

Oh, I know a lot about that. And spiritual. I know a lot about that too. Isn't it true that nice people and spiritual people don't get mad? If they are still in their body, there's a darn good chance that they do. That's a whole other conversation.

Regardless, if you succeed in covering up your angst or rage, regret, sorrow, or confusion with sweetness, then nothing will have shifted for you, and you may still get that ulcer I spoke about earlier in this book.

You'll find yourself—and that part of you that can hardly breathe—withdrawing because your self-betrayal chokes your voice. Or you could find yourself continuing to complain until there's no one there to listen anymore.

Remember, your journal will always listen and never take it personally. And, if you think it might take it personally just because it's glaring at you, write on that feeling to ease your guilt.

Check in with yourself. What irks you right now? Let it out even if it happened twenty-six years ago and is still swimming around in your liver, where, it is believed in Chinese medicine, rage is stored. Scribble, scream, cry, and release. It might take a while to get in touch with whatever you buried there.

Simply begin recording what happened from your memory. Write it the way you remember it. And, unless a bear attacks while you sit reading this, your upset is not about this present moment. It's something that happened in the past. You survived it. You can heal it. Purge it onto the paper. Then go for a refreshing walk. Take Munchkin with you. (My dog, remember?) You might even meet up with Sally Graves and her boyfriend if you happen to be in Africa. Be brave, be honest, write beyond your cunning inner editor, and see where it takes you.

WRITING PROMPT: Today, I am willing to say it all. I

_____

_____

_____

_____

_____

_____

_____

_____

_____

_____

_____

_____

_____

_____

_____

_____

_____

_____

_____

_____

_____

_____

_____

_____

_____

_____

Betrayal

Afraid someone will discover what you wrote and read it? This can be a legitimate fear when you're writing a journal or anything else meant for your eyes only. You want to protect it because it's sacred. The writings you produce are your babies, and protecting them is cherishing your innocent, tender, and creative voice. If you think someone may read what you've written, it can inhibit what you write.

On the first page of your journal, you can write, "Please, do not read this. Put it down. It is personal." Or, if you really mean business, take out the "Please." Instead, write: "PUT IT DOWN! NOW!"

If you want to be even bolder, inscribe, "Read at your own risk!" It could certainly be risky to the reader if you're disgruntled by her or him and have written all about it.

After all, you could have a totally different perspective once you got it out of your system. You may even see your participation in the event. The person reading your journal wouldn't see that part because you took off to the garden to water your flowers and count your blessings, knowing that you don't need to bring up the subject again. But she will. On burned toast mixed with a basket of weeping willow branches and dead roses.

Here's a valuable writing tip; don't leave your journal on the coffee table or anywhere else out in the open, for that matter. If you do, you can cancel your plans to go see the latest award-winning drama. You may be starring in the one you've just written with a ready-made cast of unsavoury, vengeful characters. Just sayin'.

Have you ever had your journal read or something else that was private—especially by someone you trusted? How did it make you feel? Write about it!

By the way, I did too. Twice. I was furious, hurt, frustrated, resentful and belligerent. Yet, I didn't have the tools or skills to say anything. I was shy and scared and pushed all those feelings inward and carried them deep inside me.

Don't kid yourself—I would also rage without warning or become passive-aggressive—saying one thing while, on the inside, I was seething and meaning another. Or I simply became passive and depressed.

Gratefully, after years of higher learning, therapy and practicing healthy communication skills—including writing a lot of angry, blaming letters but never sending them—I can now say I rarely dump my feelings on others. I am assertive, though, and I let people know what's going on, and I'm always open, ready, and willing to hear what's going on for them too.

And I went on to write books. So please, consider this and don't let what happened to you when someone you trusted betrayed your trust stop you from moving forward. Remember, the past does NOT equal the future. Claim your sovereignty!

WRITING PROMPT: I remember the time when someone I trusted betrayed me by reading my journal. I felt _____. Today I'm going to write them a letter which shall remain in my journal, but I will say it all.

Dear_____

Later, after, after giving it at least four or five days to settle, imagine that person heard every word you wrote, listened respectfully, and writes you a letter back from their highest self, saying...

_____

_____

_____

_____

_____

_____

_____

_____

_____

_____

_____

_____

_____

_____

_____

_____

_____

_____

_____

_____

Can't Spell or Haven't a Clue about Proper Grammar and Punctuation

I've touched on this already, but I'm saying it again because it's a fact. People stop themselves from writing because of poor spelling, punctuation, and grammar. More than you can imagine. I urge you, do not go there. Journal writing is about getting it down. Full stop. Goodbye. Sayonara. The end. Throw out your perfectionist tendencies.

My advice—whether to do with cleaning your house until it glows in the dark or wringing your hands until they do—is that writing this way makes your brain go sterile. You will kill all the antibodies desperately trying to keep their creative chums alive. Leave your left brain out of it until everything you want to get on the page is on it. Don't stop to edit while you write.

Kids paint outside the lines. You get to write outside the margins. Your ravenous left brain will get its delectable dessert later, should you decide to take your journal entries to the next level. Then you can take it to an editor. Your left brain will think it's Christmas Day or it has entered the pearly gates of heaven.

I'll tell you another secret. If you're writing about something that has deep meaning for you and stick with it, going right to the marrow and allowing it to come out raw, it often won't need much editing. Why? Because your authentic voice is what the reader wants to hear. You can leave dotting the "i's" and crossing the "t's" for a professional editor.

WRITING PROMPT: Deliberately write a few sentences with ridiculous grammar and spelling, even when you know how to write and spell. Here's an example:

"Me bee een kountree hole bunches hlonge thyme." Or "Nevr ctop writeeng, hokey?"

It's hilarious, but you know what it says. Let yourself laugh and keep going. Hoki Doki!

_____

_____

_____

_____

_____

_____

_____

_____

_____

_____

_____

_____

_____

_____

_____

_____

_____

_____

_____

_____

_____

_____

Afraid that if You Put it in Writing, You're Bound by It

There's always been an aura around the written word. It's like a law or contract that can't be changed.

"Gee, I wrote it this way, so how can I say it that way now?" Well, you can. That's poetic license. You can always change your thoughts, minds, and perceptions as you learn and grow. You can write something, stand by it today, and then change it tonight if it no longer resonates with your truth.

The irony is that as soon as you write the truth of where you are in the moment, the energy shifts and allows for other truths to seep in. You're not frozen in your fury, for example.

Once you've spilled it all onto the pages, you often hit a deeper emotion, possibly heartbreak, that's been buried until now. You discover that under the rage lies a hurt younger part of yourself who hasn't had his or her needs met.

With this awareness, you can then do some nurturing, such as writing yourself a love letter. Promise that younger you that even though you were abandoned, criticized, and bullied by so and so, you promise never to do that to your younger self. You love her or him like never before. Then, keep your promise in order to build confidence, authenticity, integrity, and a loving backbone.

It may take a while for this deeper awareness to seep in. Write and stay patient. You could be ironing a shirt one day and suddenly have an epiphany. Your partner shouts out, "Where's dinner?" Instead of having your blood boil, you call back, "I'll be right there, sweetheart." And you mean it. You weren't triggered. That's when you know you have healed that one.

An endless well of wisdom comes to us from invisible places that the pen simply knows how to locate. Allow your writing to teach you things. Learn as you write. Grow as you learn. Let it be a progression, not a fact. As I often say, "An endless well of wisdom comes to us from invisible places that the pen simply knows how to locate."

When we let it. Nothing's written in stone. And if it is, eventually, someone will pick up the stone, skip it in the water, and discover the world's not flat after all. (I'm not sure how that works, but it's true. Or not. Maybe I'll change my mind.)

WRITING PROMPT: Think of a time when you were pretty sold on something; in other words, you believed it to be true. Then something happened to change your mind. What was it? How did you come upon this new truth? Once you did, what did you do, say, think, and feel?

Or is there something niggling at you right now? You're on the fence about something. You have a sense that something is just not right about your belief, and yet you're having a hard time letting go.

Write about it. Write right through to the other side. Remember what I said above, "An endless well of wisdom comes to us from invisible places that the pen simply knows how to locate."

Remember, too, as humans, we can change our minds. Nothing is written in stone. Being flexible is key.

_____

_____

_____

_____

_____

_____

_____

_____

_____

_____

_____

_____

_____

_____

_____

_____

_____

_____

_____

_____

_____

_____

_____

_____

_____

_____

_____

Afraid of What You'll Learn About Yourself

Writing takes you into the deeper recesses of your mind, turning over the soil of the unconscious and bringing light to what's
been buried for a long time.

If you have things you don't want to face or don't want to deal
with, you will avoid writing because the truth usually surfaces and
makes you look at it. Don't be afraid. Be curious instead. When
you stay with it and write to the other side, you will gain clarity,
answers, healing, and release.

Once you have clarity, you may see your hand in some of the
things that happened to you and that you previously blamed others for. This is not an opportunity to beat yourself up. Forgive
yourself.

If that person is still in your life, consider apologizing to her
or him. If it's so long ago, and you wouldn't know how to reach
them, you can write them a letter sharing what you have since
learned. Even though you don't have an address, the act of writing
it will free you. Or simply sit quietly and send intentional loving
energy. Make sure you do it for yourself first as well. Love the parts
of you that feel bad, guilty, sorry, and regretful. Those parts need
more love, not less.

WRITING PROMPT: You are writing this to yourself. It's about you getting to know you.

What I want you to know about me is...

_____

_____

_____

_____

_____

_____

_____

_____

_____

_____

_____

_____

_____

_____

_____

_____

_____

_____

_____

_____

_____

_____

_____

_____

_____

_____

Competition

Some people stay in a state of paralysis because they are always comparing themselves to others. Do you do that? Do you say to yourself, "So and so graduated at the same time as me, wasn't half as smart, and has three books under her belt?"

Comparing yourself to others is damaging because it stops your creative flow. How often do you hear the call to create something, a book, blog, or song but stop yourself because you don't think you're good enough or that others have written on that subject already?

They probably have, but they're not you. No one can describe anything in your unique voice.

You may be asking yourself the wrong questions and getting the wrong answers. You say, "How come she can do or say it?" Or "No wonder he's successful; he has a rich father." Instead of asking yourself, "What are my goals, and what can I do today toward them?"

WRITING PROMPT: Take one writing project that you have on the go—or want to have—and get to it. There's no trick. Just roll up your sleeves and write. Once you've started, you will know the sheer joy of moving forward, motivating you to come back tomorrow, the next day, and the next day after that. And, when you get stuck, write your truth about it in your journal. It will free you, and you can continue with your project.

_____

_____

_____

_____

_____

_____

_____

_____

_____

_____

_____

_____

_____

_____

_____

_____

_____

_____

_____

_____

_____

_____

_____

Don't Know What to Say

Not knowing where to begin and staring at a blank page can sometimes feel ominous. A storm is brewing, but you can't tell from which direction it's coming. Should you take your clothes off the clothesline or eat lunch first? Or should you let the storm drench the pages in your journal until the sun comes out?

Begin right where you are. Describe what's happening. Make broad sweeps with your pen, like dipping a paintbrush into a pallet of endless colours. Even the black and blue ones.

Here's an example:

I feel stuck. No. I don't feel stuck. I am stuck. This blank page is daunting. It feels too much like my life these days. I don't want to write. But I keep telling myself I must. I must let myself scream here...allow the pages to hold my words...the words I dare not speak out loud. The silence is suffocating. The walls in this house are hollow, echoing my loneliness. Relentless loneliness. Stifled tears are hidden in the crevices. I dare not even let out a whimper lest it turns into pounding wails of grief without end. How could he leave and never come back? My heart is pounding in my chest. But at least I feel my heart. I've been depressed for so long. I've been numb, no, dead! Oh, blank page, thank you for holding my pain and churning it into something that has a heart—a heart that feels and tells me I am alive. Maybe this is the crack that lets the light in. I always loved that lyric from Leonard Cohen's song, "Anthem". I have always loved Leonard Cohen. His poetry and songs touch my heartache with his own. Well, they used to. I haven't listened to any music since the day he walked out the door. I'm going to play that song. God, I need some light to come in. And hope. God, how I need hope...

Did you notice that in the example above, I deliberately did not separate the paragraphs? No, even though there are periods, it almost reads like a run-on sentence. This is deliberate. This is how it is when you put your pen to paper and just let go of everything but allow your pen to run across the pages of your journal. You're not concerned here about paragraphs or sentence structure or whether anything is in the "right" order. You're only concerned about getting what you are feeling out of your body and onto the page. You can see how, even in this example (fictitious as a way of demonstrating how works), in very little time, the writer moved from hopelessness to potentialities to wanting to play a favourite song.

Still don't know what to write about? Write about not knowing what to write about. In fact, not knowing what to write about can be such a block that I've given you two writing prompts to work with. Here's another one of my examples:

The last time I had nothing to say, I couldn't stop talking. That's because Richard actually asked me what I was feeling. Seriously? Okay, he asked, so I told him. I didn't notice that he had vacated the conversation twenty minutes earlier while I continued sharing. Sharing. Well, some would call it that. He later called it ranting. That's after he came back from eating a plate of soup, watching the football game, drinking beer, playing a round of poker, and taking the dog for a walk. That's what he told me when I asked him where he was while I was talking. He said his mind just went to a few more pleasant places.

Still not inspired? Still stuck? All write, right, turn to Part Five for a series of suggested writing prompts and other good stuff. I've sent your muse ahead of you to meet you there. But not before your next writing exercise. You didn't think I'd let you down, did you?

First, I'm going to pretend I'm you, and I'm going to be bold and say right to your face:

"Yes, Junie, I feel stuck—yup, lots of chances to write from all the reasons why people like me hate to write—why don't you just call it like it is? It's called Writer's Block, and I have a bad case of it!"

And this is what I'd say back to you, and I'm going to be serious with you for a strict minute…

"Dig deeper. *There's no such thing as "Writer's Block."* What there is, though, for many people is F.E.A.R., False Evidence Appearing Real."

Unless there is a sabre-toothed tiger loose in your house right now, and your house has no doors, and you forgot to charge your phone to call an ambulance ahead of time, and the tiger is headed right for you—well, you simply need to take some deep breaths, move to your writing table, and WRITE! Write the truth. Write what is at the core of what's stopping you.

Probably one of the topics in this section has touched a nerve. Maybe more than one. Maybe it's something completely different. Whatever it is, don't you dare quit! You've come so far. Simply write and let go of the outcome. Don't judge, censor, or try to make it sound pretty or not as awful as it feels. Just write the truth and allow for new discoveries, new truths, and new spaciousness that before now has been blocked by fear, doubt and likely, judgment towards others and yourself. You can do this, and I'm counting on you.

WRITING PROMPT A: The last time I had nothing to say, I...

_____

_____

_____

_____

_____

_____

_____

_____

_____

_____

_____

_____

_____

_____

_____

_____

_____

_____

_____

_____

_____

_____

_____

_____

_____

_____

_____

WRITING PROMPT B: I am willing to write what's bugging me, what I think is causing me to stay stuck...

Or I am NOT willing to write down what's bugging me, no matter the cost... (anger, fear, depression, an ulcer, you get the picture)

_____

_____

_____

_____

_____

_____

_____

_____

_____

_____

_____

_____

_____

_____

_____

_____

_____

_____

_____

_____

_____

_____

_____

_____

Part Three
LET'S GO DEEPER

H ere you get the privilege of reading my answers while I get
to show off my skills and, dare I say, brilliance as a psycho-
therapist.

Common questions asked by people who say that the very
thought of writing gives them an ulcer but are still curious! Count
how many of the following questions are on your list. More than
one? You need this book. I'm delighted it's landed in your lap!

Wouldn't putting down my emotions on paper just reinforce my emotional turmoil and re-traumatize me? It's hard enough living it once!

Many people hide and repress their feelings to stay safe or keep a certain persona for the outside world. This is what causes a major amount of anxiety in the first place.

Writing your emotions and thoughts in a journal allows you to acknowledge your truth, automatically shifting the energy around. Doing so brings clarity, and you will feel much better.

How so? As you come to better understand yourself through journaling, you begin to express it in a way that feels authentic and supports who you are. All these things help to make you feel more in control of your life, which, in turn, builds confidence and self-esteem. You now know where to go from here. You've taken the first step. And the best part of all, your journal provides a sense of safety in the world.

You can rely on it. When everything else seems crazy and upside-down, the journal will turn it right-side up again. It will never reject you. It's always available when you are, and it will accept your truth in whichever way you wish to express it. Also, it honours your process; you can step tentatively into the waters or dive right in. No one's there to hurry you along.

Should I share my writing with my therapist?

Writing will enhance the talk therapy. As I have already discussed, it is a great tool to open up the subconscious mind and reveal what has been hidden, perhaps for decades. In my practice, I will ask clients to write about a specific issue they are working on. When they read it back, often there is an effect, such as anger or sadness, releasing tears that have long been buried. Writing and reading out loud to your therapist is a great starting point for further conversation and deeper exploration.

One client wrote a letter to her father, who has been dead for over a decade. It formed part of the grieving process—finally telling him some things she'd held back for a long time. She wrote about the things that she hated him for, such as leaving her and her mom when she was only four years old. She told him all the things she regretted.

Even though she still saw a lot of him during her life, she always felt like a burden and that he disapproved of her, even though he never said it out loud. She regretted that they never spent real time together. She read out loud what she'd written and released the pain that she'd carried for decades. Writing her truth gave her back her voice. When we talked about her dad a few weeks later, I asked her to write him another letter. It surprised her to see how much more at peace she felt. She wrote from a place of compassion that soon led to forgiveness.

How does journal writing translate into creative writing?

Sometimes, people associate journal writing with feelings of pain and sadness, but it is often in the process of writing this stuff that the best stories emerge.

All of us have a tremendous wealth of creativity just below the surface, doing everything it can to get our attention. I've had executive clients that saw the entire writing process as frivolous—a waste of time—but agreed to try journaling anyway. Much to their delight, each one of these people, without fail, found it moved them forward into other areas of creativity long buried. They also started to infuse personality and humour into dry, technical business reports and summaries and even looked forward to writing them.

A former writing student and stay-at-home mom, who never wrote much more than bread-and-butter notes, began journaling several years ago. Magical children's stories started appearing on the page. She started flushing them out and found the process to be fun and inspiring. Encouraged by her seven-year-old, she started reading one story at a time while fully acting out the parts at her local library's Tots and Toddler Program on Tuesday mornings. Before she knew it, she had every child's eager attention as they hung onto every word. Squeals of laughter would fill the room. Betty went from simply writing ideas down in her journal to full stories that would fill the hearts of children for long after the stories were told.

The act of journaling every day builds a foundation for all kinds of writing. As we get to know ourselves better, we're more willing to unleash our creativity, take more risks, and write that first poem, short story, play, or novel that will delight our readers and ourselves!

Supposing I'm miserable, what will writing about it do?

Writing will help you better understand yourself and bring clarity to the situations you are facing. Sometimes, things feel overwhelming because the to-do list has gotten out of hand, and writing is just one more darn thing to add to it.

While that may be true, if you're reading this book, there's a good chance your soul has been calling you to write. This would be a good time to put writing into a different category than the "To-Do List." Put it on the "To-Love List." Let it be your reward.

Writing for as little as ten minutes a day could bring about spaciousness, where you are carried from your external world of overwhelm to a quieter place within.

Allow writing to give you a place to breathe back into your centre. A place where you can rest your heart on the page with your words. You won't need to put on the "I am fine, thank you," mask, pretending all is well for those around you.

When is it safe to share my writing with others?

It's your call. However, if you want to share it with someone seeking approval, that's a red flag. It can be a healing thing to do, as long as the person with whom you're sharing is supportive of who you are—someone that sincerely cares about you and your process. Hopefully, a good friend or your partner. Also, be sure that your therapist is in that category and not someone distant and emotionally unavailable. Check in with your gut and honour your truth.

Here's something else to consider; don't write with the idea of sharing it with anyone. This could stop you dead in your tracks. You will be censoring what you're saying—writing it the way you think someone will want to hear it. You lose your authentic self this way and write only on the surface. There is no benefit to this. You're only fooling yourself. Don't do it.

It's different if you are in a writing group. That's why most people attend writing groups so they can read their writing. My groups are called *sacred writing circles*. The participants feel free to share because we do not criticize each other.

Your soul flourishes in an atmosphere of trust and safety. It shrivels and shuts down when you feel that people are judging you. If you're in a writer's group that is more about harsh critiquing, check in with yourself and see if it's really where you want to be. When it's the right mix, when you and your writing are being honoured, and when the feedback is kind and supportive, magic happens.

In his book *Personal Creativity and Writing*, Jeff Richardson asks the reader if they've ever had the experience of being heard without interruption by the other person or being judged by them. He speaks of the importance of the quality of someone's attention when they listen to you so that you feel truly and deeply heard. This is what can happen in a sacred writing circle, and for some of you, this may be the first time in your life when you experience being truly listened to. This can create the building blocks of confidence and motivation and can be a very powerful catalyst for your writing.

What if I keep writing and nothing changes?

Is this something you might say?

"I feel lousy. I've felt this way for weeks. I can't see how the writing's going to make any difference. I started, and all I'm doing is saying the same things over and over again—it's not getting any better. I'm not learning anything new." And you probably won't if you keep saying the same things. Try saying something else.

Einstein said that we cannot solve a problem with the same mind that created it. So, if you've been feeling lousy for a long time, play a game with yourself. Tell yourself that you are feeling awesome. I know that I said you should write authentically, but sometimes, we have to play the "fake it 'til we make it" game.

Pretend you are writing fiction. Make it about someone else and write a happy ending. And make the middle part happy too. Move from the quest to the critical choice.

And if it puts you into a rage that I even suggested doing that, awesome! Write about it. Get mad. But don't make it about me. You hardly know me! Well, you can if you like—but it might be more effective if you go to the underbelly of what's really bothering you. Seriously, it's me? Darn, I hate confrontation!

Okay, if everything I am saying here is annoying, jot it down and go for a walk. Get some fresh air. It's like alchemy. It can transform annoyance into "What's the big deal?" Come home and write about that!

Or another option or two, simply have compassion for the part of you that resists change and let it be. Love that part of yourself. Then be still and ask inside for guidance. My educated guess is you'll get some.

Fine, but what if I simply hate writing?

Well, if none of the above, or anything else I've written in this book, has inspired you to pick up your pen, then you can book an emergency appointment with a shrink or take up sky diving or underwater discovery instead. That should motivate you. Or simply forget the idea and burn this book. Then let your friends know that you did that on Facebook and Twitter, Instagram and TikTok. Make sure you say whose book it is. It'll go viral. Everyone will want to read it. I'll become famous! And prosperous! I'll buy you dinner. If you don't care to take such drastic steps and you're not into burning books, try the next chapter or turn to Part Five.

Part Four
Writing Prompts, Tips & Brilliant Ideas

Have a Dialogue with Your Inner Child

When we feel hurt, angry, or afraid, we will often resort to behaviours and reactions that can be less than effective. We might project our rage onto others who are not responsible for our feelings or find some instant-gratification self-soothing habit not to feel the emotion at all.

This is an excellent time to talk to your inner child, who is the one who needs your attention. Using a pen with your dominant hand, representing you, the adult, ask your little girl or boy to tell you how she or he feels, and truly listen. Have your inner child choose a coloured crayon with your non-dominant hand to respond.

When I first did this exercise many years ago, it went something like this:

Me: "How are you, sweet little Junie?"

Child: (She picks up a black crayon and scribbles) "Why would you care?"

Me: "Of course I care."

Child: "You do not, and I hate you!"

Me: "I am so sorry I have hurt you this much. How old are you, sweetheart?"

Child: "I'm seven."

Me: "Where are you?"

Child: "I'm under the bed."

Me: "Why are you there? Are you frightened?"

Child: (Grabs black crayon and in capital letters) "I'M NEVER COMING OUT!"

Me: "Do you want to talk about it, honey?"

Child: "NO! You never listen!"

As we continued our dialogue, I learned that the child in me was screaming on the inside to leave the man I was living with, that he was controlling and that I had let him take over our lives, and she never had a voice.

I promised I would listen, love her more, and commit to her more than ever. I did my best to keep that promise. It didn't happen right away—I guess that I needed some more sledgehammers first.

So, I renewed my promise and would show up every day on the page and invite her in. I let her speak her truth. I gave her back her voice. My voice—my voice of vulnerability and fear that I hid from because I didn't want to face the fact that she was right. I so wanted the relationship with the man I was with to work out.

My dialogue with that vulnerable part of me showed me in living colour what it was costing me to stay in an abusive relationship. Eventually, I got the courage to leave. I gave myself the gift of loving the part of me that I had buried for so long. I stopped abandoning myself. It all started in my journal with loving, acknowledging, and listening deeply to the voice that knew the truth all along.

WRITING PROMPT: Gather your notebook, and coloured markers, choose a time when you are alone and will be uninterrupted for the next hour and write to that sweet, loving child of yours. Let him or her know you are there for them. Often that part of us is very vulnerable and will show it in various ways. Some become quiet, silent, and unable to express their truth. Possibly that younger part has become rebellious instead. Let them have their say; be loving, compassionate, and open no matter what. Using my example above, begin to have a dialogue: Remember to use your dominant hand, representing you, the adult, when asking your little girl or boy to tell you how she or he feels. Have your inner child choose a coloured crayon and write their reply with your non-dominant.

Dear _____ (use the name you were called when you were a child)

Remember to use your dominant hand, representing you, the adult, when asking your little girl or boy to tell you how she or he feels. Have your inner child choose a coloured crayon and write their reply with your non-dominant.

_____

_____

_____

_____

_____

_____

_____

_____

_____

_____

_____

_____

_____

_____

_____

_____

_____

_____

_____

_____

_____

_____

_____

_____

_____

_____

_____

Ask for Guidance

You can use your journal to ask for guidance from God, your Higher Power, the Universe, or Harry, your next-door neighbour, without him ever knowing. Personally, I'd go for a supreme being, so I don't go and beat up Harry if I take the advice I just channelled from him, and it was a complete waste of time. Seriously, asking for guidance from God, the angels and guides, or my Higher Self is one of my favourite things to do. And I encourage you to do it too. I do it with sincerity and humility and always get an answer. Maybe not right away, but it comes. It comes on the page or from an unexpected source.

WRITING PROMPT: Dear _____, Please, give me guidance regarding _____. I am at a loss and need your help…

Open yourself to receive.

_____

_____

_____

_____

_____

_____

_____

_____

_____

_____

_____

_____

_____

_____

_____

_____

_____

_____

_____

_____

_____

_____

_____

_____

_____

_____

_____

_____

The Angry, Blaming Letter

Although I have already given an example of this earlier in my letter to my teacher, Miss Simmons, I feel it bears repeating because it's one of the most effective antidotes for emotions you are feeling but are keeping inside or expressing in ways that are not serving you well. And it is 100% safe as long as you don't put it in an email and press send!

Write a blaming, angry, and uncensored letter. It's a safe and healthy way of getting your rage out of your body and onto sheets of paper that won't get angry back. By the time you're ready to deal directly with the person, you will be feeling much calmer and more centred. You'll likely have a deeper understanding of what's underneath the anger.

Often, it's fear or sadness. As you continue to stay with this process, you'll discover that your feelings have nothing to do with the person with whom you feel angry. They're usually from a much earlier time in your life, and this person triggered your unhealed wounds.

Until you heal these wounds, you'll continue to project your anger, hurt, pain, fear, etc., onto the people in your life. As you heal and grow, you can look back and see these opportunities for forgiveness, healing, and growth.

Follow this thread to its origin in your past if you can. Stay with it, remembering not to embody these memories. When you have completed your writing, put your pen down and take a brisk walk out in nature, or put on some music and move your body with wild abandon! Notice if your reaction to the person who initially triggered but who reminds you of someone else has decreased. If not, return to your writing and continue to write into the truth of how the person in the present reminds you of the person from your past while reclaiming your power back on the page of what is true for you. Changing your state of mind will help expedite the healing of both the past and present situations.

WRITING PROMPT: Take the time to be quiet and think about someone in your life that somehow triggers you when you think about them; for example, you feel anger, pain, resentment or fear. Now ask for guidance about whom this person reminds you of from when you were younger. Be willing to sit in the discomfort of this while you put pen to paper.

When I think of _____, I feel upset. They remind me of_____. I remember when…

_____

_____

_____

_____

_____

_____

_____

_____

_____

_____

_____

_____

_____

_____

_____

_____

_____

_____

_____

_____

Excellent Writing Tips to Help You Stay on Target

Mind Mapping

This is a fun and effective method to use before writing a book, blog, poem, article, play, or any creative endeavour that you are planning.

There is no structure or form. It's free-association brain-storming using your right brain. Right-brain activity uses pictures, symbols, and images and is non-verbal. It is the part of our nature that is intuitive, sensuous, artistic, and spontaneous. It works with shapes and patterns.

While writing, simply be open to receiving. You are a conduit, not a planner. This is what the left-brain function does. It is verbal, linear, logical, rational, and cognitive. This is the part of the brain we want to engage when we are ready to go back and edit. It is not what we want to activate during the creative process. There is a myriad of ways to mind map. Google it and choose one that feels right for you.

You can use my Mind Map as a reference for drawing your own. In my book, *Your Life Matters: 8 Simple Steps to Writing Your Story*, I use this tool to help people write their memories. Once it's flushed out, it becomes the working outline for the book's chapters and subchapters.

Mind Map

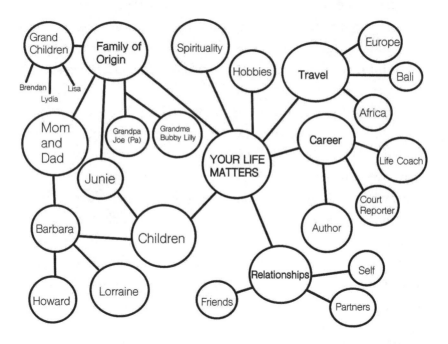

Be Surprised

Write for no reason at all. Check out Julia Cameron's Morning Pages, that she writes about in her book, *The Artist's Way: A Spiritual Path to Higher Creativity*. Morning Pages are three 8 1/2 X 11 pages that you write every morning in long-hand. It's not about fabulous writing. It's writing for the sake of writing. It may start off as a shopping list—all your To-Do's for that day. Don't be surprised if your sentences start to shape themselves differently and poetry flows out of your pen instead. I love using crisp white paper for this exercise and my favourite pen. When I'm done, I put my pages into a binder that I keep for this specific type of writing.

Keep Your Journal with You at All Times

Well, I can think of some exceptions. "Will you turn on the light, honey, and pass me my journal? I need to capture that stunning orgasm on paper for a contest I entered on erotic writing." It may be the last piece of writing you ever write with that particular lover.

What I had in mind was more in line with jotting down story ideas or writing a poem while waiting in the dentist's office. Ray Bradbury, in *Zen in the Art of Writing*, says that if you don't write every day, you risk accumulating unsaid words, ideas and stories and that you'd begin to die a little each day or take up acting!

But maybe, you can be more discerning about when. Just sayin'.

What's Music Got to Do with It?

Try it without. Find what's right for you. It could be lyrical, jazzy, upbeat, mellow, familiar, unfamiliar, drumming, or rap. Experiment.

I always thought I needed absolute quiet while I was writing. That was until I was writing my book, *Re-Write Your Life*. I was spending so much time alone; I was craving to be out in the world. Writing can be a lonely endeavour.

So, I skipped off to Serious Coffee with my laptop (seriously, it's called Serious Coffee), and the hum in the background seemed to help keep me focused or entertained or in a better mood because there was life stirring around me. Not sure what it was. All I know is that I stayed focused. Every now and again, I would look up and notice it was packed in there. And it was loud, and the cappuccino maker was screeching, and I'd say to myself, "Wow! Is it ever noisy in here!"...and carry on writing. I can't say it's happened every time since, but I have let go of the myth that I need silence to write.

Breathe

Writing is a whole-body exercise, not just the hands and brain. The more grounded you are in your body, the deeper your writing will be. In life, when we are scared, our breathing becomes shallow. The same thing happens when we are writing something disturbing. Our writing tends to linger on the surface. When this happens, just take some deep breaths, and keep going. It's okay. Writing the truth won't hurt you. Not writing it could, though.

In his book, *Writing from the Body*, John Lee reminds the reader of how powerful their body's knowledge is and that you must welcome your emotions completely. Lee talks about using your breath to bring forward what needs to be expressed by let-ting the pen follow your breath. So, take a deep breath, and write where you are.

Write Without Stopping

Keep your hand always moving. If you notice your hand in the air or on your lap, or somewhere else other than the page, you're probably thinking about something instead of writing it down. Or you're judging what you have just written. Thinking is not allowed. It invites your inner monster to come out and say mean things to you, like, "Don't you have better things to do?" and "Who are you trying to impress?" If you just keep on writing, 'the voice' doesn't have a chance to ruin your life. It comes to life in long pauses, so don't give it any!

Forget the Rules You Learned in School (but please don't tell your teacher I said so)

If you want to learn how to punctuate properly, understand syntaxes, or where to place paragraphs, what to do with run-on sentences, how to identify subordinate clauses and expletives, position prepositions, learn the use of emphatic forms of active voice, overworked adjectives, modifiers, and other things along that vein (did I actually write that!), I suppose there are dozens of English classes that could teach you. Not me. I wouldn't know what to tell you. So, I won't. You don't need any of it in your journal. It's the process and not perfection that we're interested in.

Find a Writing Buddy

Commit to meeting once a week, doing timed writings together, and then sharing what you wrote. It will keep you motivated, and the support that you give and receive will prove invaluable.

Be sure to put it in your calendar and commit to it. Remember, you don't have to do this alone.

Creating a Sacred Writing Space

There's nothing like having welcoming, friendly, and beautiful surroundings to inspire you to write. It doesn't have to be big, just inviting. Make it yours. Light a candle. Place your favourite flowers on the table or add a picture of someone precious to you that you can imagine smiling and comforting you as you write.

Magazines Aren't Just for Reading, You Know

Cut out pictures that catch your attention: Write what comes from looking at them. You'll be amazed. Often, in life, what we see and hear—pictures and images and tones of voices—speak to us, but we don't take the time to listen to what they're saying. You'll uncover hidden meanings as to why you chose a picture once you start writing about it.

False Endings

When you're doing timed writing and are writing quickly but want to stop before the time is up because you think you have nothing more to say or you're judging it as being stupid or not good enough or something else, just put two diagonal lines on the page where you want to stop, like this: // and then continue writing.

You can repeat the last sentence you wrote again and again if need be. Eventually, it will change into something else. This is a way of busting through writer's block, which usually comes from self-judgment. Later, when you read what you have written, don't be surprised if, just beyond the diagonal lines, what comes next is writing you are totally impressed with—inspiring insights, metaphors, ideas, poetry, etc.

Some of my best writing has come after I thought I wanted to quit and pushed past my resistance, and continued anyway. But not always. Expect miracles to happen; expect nothing in particular, but you won't know if you don't check it out.

Read Lots

Listening to people who are good models of speech helps us to speak well; reading good models of writing inspires us to write. Keep a list of topics in the back of your journal to write about when your imagination has gone fishing: Or take a few from the ones I've listed in Part Five and put them on your plate. Not too many at once, though. They could cause indigestion or writer's block if there were such an animal.

Part Five
NO MORE EXCUSES: WRITING TOPICS I PROMISED YOU

Which ones do you resonate with? Put the title on the page and begin writing. Don't go into your head and try to figure out why you chose it. You chose it because you chose it. There are lots, so maybe you should just close your eyes and point so you don't get stuck choosing.

And, once you've written your stories, if you like, you can send them to Junie's Writing Sanctuary on Facebook to share with other writers just like yourself. You'll find the link in the Resources section at the back of the book.

Writing Prompts, Topics, and Themes

Put a checkmark beside the ones you want to write about.
1. I remember the hour when...
2. Write the story of a teacher, mentor or friend in your life who influenced you the most...
3. It doesn't matter that...
4. "Sorry, just doesn't cut it," she or he said...
5. I used to pass that street every day. Now...
6. How did you fantasize about your life when you were eight years old and write from that voice...
7. I let the fire die because...
8. If I were willing to be vulnerable, I...
9. Describe the perfect day from the moment you open your eyes in the morning...
10. It couldn't have been a more inconvenient time when...
11. Patience is not empty waiting. It's inner certainty...
12. Play a song and then write what it invokes in you...
13. If I could make anything disappear, I...
14. Recall an important memory from your childhood and tell it from the perspective of someone else who was present...
15. What I need most to change is...
16. What matters most now is...
17. The last words she said to me were...
18. If I could do it over, I would...
19. I am grateful because...
20. Write about an item you have that isn't expensive but means a lot to you...
21. The greatest gift I ever received was...
22. Describe everything about a street you once lived on, the people, the vibe...

23. You have entered a time machine going back and forward in time...
24. My greatest desire is...
25. I contribute best when...
26. I promised I wouldn't look back...
27. I had to lie because...
28. How will I ever trust after...
29. I know I am the creator of my life because...
30. I am the happiest when...
31. Describe someone you adore...
32. My favourite family memory is...
33. What haunts me still is...
34. I can't seem to let go of...
35. I refuse to stay silent any longer...
36. What feeds my soul is...
37. Writing brings out the truth, and I'm afraid to acknowledge...
38. I am sick of being "nice! I want to...
39. Dear God...
40. I love it when...
41. The song that takes me to my favourite childhood memory is...
42. When my mom...
43. A lie that I said that I have never forgotten is...If that situation happened today, I would...
44. Once upon a time, there was a little girl/boy who...
45. I choose to...
46. In the spring, I...
47. In the summer, I...
48. In the fall, I...
49. In the winter, I...

50. My friend showed up for me when…
51. I love my quiet time because…
52. My favourite form of creative self-expression is…
53. When I am creative I…
54. I am an enlightened being because…
55. What I have learned in my _____years is _____
and what I know for sure is…

Part Six
FROM JOURNALS TO JEWEL

One of the most delightful and unexpected surprises my journal showed me was that its entries would often become the springboard to many other writing genres. Some of my darkest entries became poetry, short stories, plays, and songs. Countless students over the years have also moved from their journals, where they were able to write the unbidden and unapologetic truths in any given moment, to then later crafting those same missives into award-winning novels, songs, and personal memoirs. They were able to transcend the hidden words in their diary into empowered conversations with some of the most important people in their lives.

Not all journal entries become award-winning something or others—nor should it be the intention going into it. Just write, as this book suggests, and write where you are! Don't try to 'make it' be anything at all. Just let the writing do the writing while you keep your hand moving along the page and allow yourself to be pleasantly surprised.

Some of my greatest achievements from writing in my journal was simply that I did it. I use my journal as a private place to let off steam in a mature and responsible way. No, truthfully, what I write may not have been neither mature nor responsible. What it is, is real. The fact that I am using my journal as my private place to spill my guts is the responsible bit. I had enough days in my youth that were laden with drama because I just said whatever I was thinking without a filter to whomever it was that I was mad at. Not a good choice. Your journal can carry everything you need to say and more.

That is why I can confidently say that when the sweet whisperings of your soul meet you on the page, and something shifts. You strengthen. You begin to stand taller. Then one day, you notice that your voice on the page becomes your voice in the world.

Below are examples from my life that began as journal entries and ended up as articles or plays, letters and short stories or a place to simply re-visit to remember the time when…

- Dearest Arny, If You Only Knew…
- In This Peace
- Lioness of the Sea
- Living with a Mental Illness: Opening to Grace
- *Madness, Masks and Miracles*
- The Phobia Song
- Remembering Papa
- Living Spaces
- Where Did It Go?

Dearest Arny, If You Only Knew...

The following letter is one among many that will be included in my new book If You Only Knew...A Book of Letters. It is dedicated to Arny Wiskin. Arny was a boy I knew in grade school, and from first appearances, you may think that his influence on my life was not more than child's play, and yet, not so. It was so much more. His kindness acted as a level gauge in my heart—a reliable anchor to hold on to—to measure others against when I was forming relationships.

Dearest Arny,

I close my eyes and see myself gazing out my window at the park. I was six when we moved to 57 Neptune Drive. It was an open field with scattered patches of weeds and grasses.

There were rabbit holes, ant hills and mice nests. At night, when it was still, you could hear the frogs and crickets. That was until the cranes showed up one day. They tore everything that was alive out of there to put down manicured lawns with swings and teeter-totters. It was OK, but I had to get used to it. The field was my first taste of freedom, and it's where I remember you the most.

My bedroom window held the perfect vantage point for looking out to see who was there at any given moment. On days when I felt anxious and insecure, looking out at my friends in the park provided me with a sense of still being connected. Even though I wasn't with them, there was something good about knowing they were there.

It was here, Arny, that I often observed you. I felt a kinship with you. We were both eleven years old. Looking now through my young girl's eyes, I see you there. It's raining outside, and you are on the swing going back and forth and back and forth slowly, always slowly. The rain is washing over you, yet you don't seem to notice or care. You've been there an hour already, and I wonder what you are thinking. How come you are not at home where it's warm and dry? I want to go and get you and bring you inside, but I don't dare. We were both so shy, and I didn't know what to say.

My young heart ached for you. I felt your loneliness in my bones. It lingered there next to my own. Although we never spoke the words, I know that somehow, we felt safe with each other. I would look over at you across the aisle from me, sitting at your little brown desk in Miss Stewart's class, drawing pictures.

You drew airplanes and cars. Detailed, precise. Perfect replicas of the models. I could see how beautiful they were. Sometimes Miss Stewart would catch you unaware and shout at you just like she used to do with me when I was daydreaming. I can't remember; did she stomp over to you, grab your beautiful pictures, and crumble them up? Did she rip your heart out as she did mine every time she made me stay after class to tell me how stupid I was? Yes, I can bet that your tender heart was torn apart with the desecration of your quiet renderings. I know mine was. Every time she hurt you, I wept.

At other times from my bedroom window, I watched you run. You ran the full circumference of the park. You made it into a race track, running round and round, picking up speed each time. Sometimes I couldn't even tell if it was you because you were indistinguishable from the trees across the way. But of course, as soon as you stopped, I knew it was you because you would take up residence once again on the swing, gently swaying back and forth, not violently like when you were running. On the swing, you caught your breath after running faster than any imaginary monster in your mind could catch up to. It was just a slow and steady back and forth. Back and forth.

Were you able to make them disappear? Did they fly out into the wind as you picked up speed? Who were those monsters, Arny? Who was it that haunted you? You were determined to beat them.

Beyond the park, you won every single track and field race. You became the fastest runner in all the city competitions. You put your mind to something and knew how to make it happen. But you never bragged. In fact, you rarely ever spoke.

Do you remember the time when we were in Grade 3, and I chose you to be Peter in the Peter Pan skit? You tried to say no, but I must have badgered you until you reluctantly said, "Okay." I played Wendy. We had our little scripts. Sometimes on my way to school, having crossed the creek that led to the path onto Baycrest Avenue, I would spot you up ahead. I would run and catch up and, with hopeful expectancy, ask,

"So, Arny, did you memorize your lines yet?"

You wouldn't answer. You just walked in the slow way you did, head down.

"Com'on Arny, did you? Did you?" I knew you hadn't, but I wouldn't let up. Eventually, if I didn't stop pestering you, you would shake your head which seemed to hang down even lower now, and whisper, "Sorry."

Now, being totally insensitive, I would cry out, "But Arny, we've only got two days left. You've got to do it. You've got to!"

I can't remember if you did learn them or not. The memory that stands out the most is that my mother took me to the hairdresser the night before the skit. My long, beautiful hair was now a short pixie cut. I could have played your part. I looked more like Peter Pan than you did!

Another time I'm sure I tortured you was when we were nine or ten years old, and I made you write something in my autograph book. You wrote this: "Roses are red, violets are green. My face is funny, but yours is a scream."

That was one of the few times you showed a sense of humour, but I didn't see it that way. I couldn't believe you wrote such a mean thing to me. I was mortified. I wanted you to show me in writing how much you liked me, so I made you write another one. You sighed but did it anyway. This time you wrote: "Roses are red, violets are green, my face is funny, but yours is a nice-lookin' sort of face."

Oh, Arny, how it makes me smile to think of you. It also makes me sad to think I picked on you so much. Was that my way awkward way of showing you I liked you?

You were a gentle boy. And you became a gentleman.

Later, on my sixteenth birthday, I had the shock of my life. The doorbell rang. I opened it only to find a gorilla that started belting out happy birthday with the most amazing voice! Those were the years of singing telegrams. When the song was over, the person with the remarkable voice removed his gorilla head, and it was none other than you! You, the boy who was so shy. How was this possible? And more than that, I never knew you could sing! Yet I did know that you pushed the edges. Maybe more than most people. Life challenged you, and you challenged it back, and you won. You always seemed to win—at least on the outside. I often wondered what was going on, on the inside. Had you ever known happiness?

Many years later, I was attending a wedding. When I went up to dance, I looked up at the stage, and there you were at the microphone, so handsome in your tuxedo, engaging the guests with your warmth. You were not only the MC but also the leader of the band. Your band! The Arny Wiskin Band. My heart swelled with happiness for you. As time went on, you became the most sought-after wedding and Bar Mitzvah band in Toronto.

Who would have ever guessed that the little boy who was too shy to learn lines for a skit, drew cars and airplanes to tune out the teachers, sat alone swinging back and forth for hours in the rain, would become a world-class athlete and performer? But you did.

I remember running into you years later. We went for a coffee. You seemed quiet and shy again. We both were. I felt I hardly knew you and in another way, I felt as though I was inside your skin. Just like it felt when I would watch you from my bedroom window all those years ago. So familiar and yet so distant at the same time.

It was awkward being with you again as an adult and our youth long gone. I had no words to bridge the gap. I thought about other men I had known. The bad boys. The ones I seemed to attract back then. And worse, fell for them, only to have my heart broken over and over.

I realized then that I had loved you. But I was too young and too scared to know what to say or to know how to be with a man such as you, a man so pure of heart.

God Bless you, Arny, wherever you are.

Addendum: My friend Kelly called me tonight, and I shared your story with her.

She said, "Hey, why don't you find Arny on Facebook or Google and establish contact again."

I couldn't believe I hadn't thought of that. I got so excited to learn where you were and be in contact again. After a long search, in utter shock, I found your obituary.

"WISKIN, Arnie - Passed away peacefully on July 6, 2009, at home..."

They mentioned family members, so I knew it was you, and I am so saddened by this news. Devastated if you want to know the truth. How I wished I could have told you what was in my heart long ago. While you were still alive.

So, dearest Arny, this story is a small token of my love. My heart would run over with joy to know that wherever you are, you are still singing.

God Bless You,

Junie

"In This Peace"

My husband, David, was concerned about me. I was unable to sleep most nights and was operating on empty.

After Covid began, having lost my 'in-person' book coaching business, I had to dance as fast as I could to find a way to get it online and then find people to register. Two things I find the most frustrating—tech and marketing!

With the help of dedicated people, I managed both. The week before my Author Mentorship Program was to begin, with eighteen people registered, I chose to take a much-needed holiday to a twenty-six-acre retreat centre cradled by two lakes with forest trails throughout. It would require taking a ferry from Victoria to Vancouver, then driving about two hours and then hopping on another ferry at Horseshoe Bay to Bowen Island, a tiny, remote island off the Coast of Vancouver Island.

David drove me there but had to return home the next day. That night, nestled in our cabin in the woods, I woke at 4:50 a.m. in absolute turmoil wanting the world to go away! I needed more than four days—I needed to get off the treadmill for at least a month.

I knew it was impossible. I had to show up and facilitate my new online program. I couldn't sleep, so went over to my computer to check some details of the course and woke David in the process.

Quietly but still frustrated, I returned to bed. David sat up and stated, "Junie, if you don't take advantage of this time here and breathe in the peace of this land, I will take your computer and your cell phone when I leave." I told him I would hide his car keys. He stayed silent awhile, then offered me what he knew would be the sure "fix" that would transform my anxiety and funk. He reached over, handed me my journal, and said, "Here, Junie, now write." I didn't want to. I wanted to whine.

Belligerently, I got out of bed, went over to the small desk, put on the desk lamp, lit a candle, and wrote from the prompt he offered me, In this peace, I shall….

And as always, I was so grateful that I did. How else will I ever know the truth? I cannot. It's writing that brings me home to myself, without fail, each and every time.

"In This Peace"

In this peace, I shall find God.
In this peace, I shall find me.
In this peace, I will unravel. I will twist and turn and be shoved and shaken, and in this peace, I shall not resist.

I will not hang onto rugged branches that jut out from the banks. I will not grasp onto their temporary refuge from the raging rapids. No, I shall let the river take me to and fro—winding down and around its billowing unpredictable forcefield.

I surrender here fully even though my heart is pumping faster than hurricane blood –coursing, exploding through this body's fragile temple—lungs infused with God's purest prana and I know even throughout this unstoppable force—leading me to destinations unseen, unknown and unchartered, never before have I felt this safe.

In these rapids I shall find peace that surpasses all understanding, and I shall rest here. Here I AM, the eye of the storm. An impartial witness in waters gone mad, born of lost dreams and uncertainty. Yet I AM Still. I AM Peace.

Did I really think my puny hands, no matter how tightly I clenched them, would save me? Such naivete.

I am ready to see, feel and know myself as the God I AM. I AM ready to drop the scales from my eyes and open them as a newborn baby does, seeing the world and its majestic splendor for the very first time.

I AM that baby. Born anew. Curious, joyful, unstoried, free! Yes, the raging rapids of my life could have bounced and broken me against a million boulders, smashed me into shards of glass, rendering me defeated, hopeless, dead even.

Instead, the waters in all their compassionate glory opened their arms to this inner river's untamed fury—infusing the turmoil with gentle, rocking motion—a lullaby quieting the unrelenting noise—the torture chamber of the mind shapeshifting me from high alert into unsuspecting emptiness and grace. Pure exhaustion finally surrendered itself, its last grasp of holding on only to arrive naked upon pristine beaches. Mother Earth's welcoming breast seducing me into deep peaceful slumber washing clean all that went before.

And when I woke it was as though a thousand nights had passed. Rested. Restored, Rendered Brand New bearing witness to Heaven on Earth.

Here I vowed to walk with the angels and saints who carried me here. I vowed to remain humble in this glorious land of Eden. Here I now taste the palate of milk and honey ready to savour its gifts in sustainable ways.

And I shall walk among others who have survived bruises too horrific to name. They too had raging river rapids now transformed into calm blue seas and it is here that we meet and recognize one another—Our Tribe—and it is our mission to walk together to shine our Gratitude, our Love and our Light. We walk fearlessly hand in hand into storms, calming the seas of disquiet for all those ready to walk among us and know the Promise and the Peace of God that beats our collective hearts as One.

In this Peace, we walk together, cocreating with our Maker.

In this Peace, we find Truth.

In this Peace, we are One.

In this Peace, we are Love.

In this Peace, we are Home.

Lioness of the Sea

This piece was written from a writing prompt, "Blessing the Boats," a poem by Louise Clifton. I placed my pen upon the pages of my journal and wrote:

"Lioness of the Sea."

I am walking along the ocean just blocks from my apartment in James Bay—the place I have called home for three years. A wonderful, glorious little community—the best place in Victoria to live as far as I am concerned, and there is nowhere else I'd rather be. So, here I am, walking along the cliffs of Dallas Rd. They aren't very high above the sea, but I've never been able to judge distance. It could be metres or feet or yards, and I don't know the difference, and it doesn't bother me. There are pathways from the highest level that lead you down to the rocky shore. Here the rocks are gray and large, and the tiny pebbles slumbering between them get washed away from their hiding place by great waves of water, burying them deeply onto the ocean floor before they have time to protest.

And today, the ocean is wild. It is chilly outside, and I zip up my bright yellow shell as far as it will go. But it doesn't go far enough, and the string at the top is broken, so I have no protection. I didn't wear a scarf. But that's okay. It's the jacket that Nathalie gave me when she stayed here last year. I love it just because it was hers, but it's not practical. I get drenched when it rains. But to its credit, I have to say it gives excellent protection from the wind on days like today.

And I love these days. I love it when the ocean is beyond taming. There is a resurgence of life—of fire raging inside the sea—a livid lioness roaring its authority across the waters and beyond the hollows of time—reminding us to behold.

Behold that there is so much more than our little minds would tell us. So much more than the killing fields that wash away the goodness and potentiality for harmony, compassion, peace, and ecstatic beauty. "I am weary," she says. "I weep for my waters and all that I have birthed beneath your world of soil because we live in fear of annihilation. Though I am weary, you haven't heard the last of my roar. I will not go leave quietly. Heed these words, you must humble yourself, humanity."

Yes, here on the shore of this raging sea, its force and power surge fiercely through my veins, ordering energy you cannot ignore. It has pushed against my thoughts, bringing me into the immediacy of this moment. I am compelled to stand still. I do, and in that moment, I am consumed with an existential knowingness that the sea is me. I rest on the clouds and watch as it splashes and soaks my face so wet and threatens to eat me whole, but even my body is not afraid. Every cell is vibrating with the electrifying presence of God in Action.

But I am aware of my body, my humanness, and I wrap my arms around it, wishing I was wearing a warm sweater under my yellow jacket because the cold chill distracts me. I want nothing to take me away from the oneness I experience with the unpretentious, unafraid, blustering roar of the lioness as her mane surges over the surface of the swells, imploring us as she growls, "Notice me! Notice how powerful I am, and if it pleases me, I can devour you in the next blink of your eye."

And those were the thoughts that penetrated my awareness as an enormous hungry swell surged over the shoreline, leaving me drenched under that useless yellow shell. I laughed. Oh, how I howled and laughed to know the truth of how in less than a blink of an eye, faster than one inhalation, I could be annihilated. But why in the world would I laugh? And the answer came as quickly as the question was asked.

I laugh because of my pompous silliness to believe I have the power to change my destiny if it's God's will when my last exhalation shall take place. But it won't be here, and it won't be today. Of that, I have become certain.

Because the ocean, as wild as she is, miraculously sees me. Sees ME. A lone woman beside the sea but who is paying attention. And in the breath that comes to me next, I feel the bond of mutual understanding and deep respect. I feel her heart in mine. She doesn't feel threatened because I have laid down my pretentious sword. The one that I've carried within a heart of sorrow. Sorrow for a lost humanity fighting against the gentleness of creation. And with the letting go come healing tears…and the Lioness cries with me. And I can't tell if the liquid salt that runs down my cheeks is hers or mine.

They are ours. Shared tears of compassionate Sacred Oneness.

(At this point, the writing became more personal… from a relationship formed by a human and lioness of the sea to the loss of a friendship. This writing became the catalyst for helping me to heal the existential pain I have always felt for the earth's desperate plight to be loved and respected. As well this journal piece was a catalyst to help me heal the anguish I carried in my heart for the loss of my friend Nikki and to forgive myself for my actions that brought it about.

This piece demonstrates my "Write Where You Are" process, where you allow the pen to take you where it will. You do not need to "stay on topic" or go in a particular order. Simply let the writing do the writing and take you where it will.

I continue to weep. But the weeping becomes more personal. I am no longer the ocean. I am a woman standing at the shore of the sea. I weep because of the loss of Nikki.

We used to walk along these shores—these rocks and the sand at dusk and at sunset. We walked when the waters were placid, and we walked when the sea was raging, like today. We'd stop to watch the herons and the gulls. And those little birds who run along the sand. We'd watch otters and seals, and we'd beach comb together. Nikki carefully choosing the pieces of driftwood that would become, through artful carving, headless goddesses that adorned her garden. I would find gratitude stones. The ones that have a circle around their centre. Sometimes I kept them, sometimes, I'd express my gratefulness and throw them into the sea. Or I'd give one to Nikki.

And we'd walk. We would share our secrets and giggle. We'd share our pain and hold each other when tears stained our cheeks. I remember more of those times than the giggles. It would be me nurturing her or her nurturing me, and there were times when we walked in silence, simply holding space. Sometimes, when there was time to spare, we'd leave the beach, walk the few blocks into the village, and drink lattes. Sometimes we were so engrossed in conversation that with a start, realizing the hour, Nikki would run to catch the next ferry back to her little island, Salt Spring—back to the bird farm where she lived with Art.

But I judged Nikki, and I'm sure she felt it. I didn't understand her. I did my best to stay open-minded even though our philosophies of loving relationships were almost diametrically opposed. But I wasn't always successful. Somehow her choices threatened me, and one of them caused the end of a friendship that spanned all the years I've lived on this coast.

I saw her yesterday. I gave the meditation at the church. She came afterwards. At tea time. It was obvious she chose not to be there during my meditation. At least, that's the story I've told myself. We spoke. Well, niceties...hello...and it was awkward.

The sea is raging again and has catapulted me back to her shores. The lioness senses my fear, beckoning me away from my ego's thoughts of Nikki. I have no choice but to abide because I know her force. Yet her roar is subsiding. And before my eyes, the impossible happened. It's beyond peculiar as I watch her shapeshift into a sandbox with a shovel and pail. How could this be? Here I am, on an ocean shore that stretches as far as the eye can see, and I have been handed a sandbox with a child's shovel and pail.

Before she changed form, her paws extended above the sea swells, and she dropped these items gingerly into my lap. I look up. Her eyes are gentle and smiling. I realize I must be dreaming as I watch her melt and disappear back into the sea—no longer raging—simple, even tides rolling peacefully onto the shore, bringing with it a majestic but mysterious silence. No sound. Nothing. Only me and my sandbox, and I am four years old.

I am in a backyard. I don't know whose it is...I don't know where I am, really. But I am alone with my yellow shovel and red pail. I fill the pail with sand, pack it down tightly with my little hands, and turn it upside down to make a castle. I am building a castle made from dreams. And now I watch her from somewhere above.

Lioness of the sea, what is this you have given me? Where have you brought me to? Why am I a little child playing in a sandbox? I don't really know that little girl.

She seems so sad. She seems lonely. I don't know how to play with her. I don't know what to say. I want to comfort her, but I don't...well, I just don't know what's going on. I'm confused.

Is she me? I imagine she is. And this pail and shovel and sand-box? What do they mean? I feel the sea inside me, and she whispers the answer in my ear. I am told these are my gifts. These are my tools. My building blocks that create anything I want. The sandbox is endless creativity. The shovel is the carver's knife. And the pail is my safe container.

Yes, Lioness. Yes, I am that child. I recognize her now, and I see that most of the castles I have built from dreams have been on sand, and the sea has swallowed them. But I am not that four-year-old girl anymore. She's in me, of that there is no doubt. But she has grown. For a brief moment, I was ready to misinterpret what I saw because I was looking through an old lens...and about to retell an old story. But the woman who was once the lonely child is no longer lonely.

Nor is she unhappy. She is contemplative. And she is building a strong foundation this time. The castle she's building is as sturdy as the pyramids and is meant to live beyond time. She knows she is safe now. She has carved many, many rooms in her castle.

She is an artist, and every day she makes inspired changes here and there. The paints on her canvas continue to change colour and shape. And sometimes, while she is sculpting from an imagination of all that is possible, the lioness reappears.

Today is such a day. She has returned to remind her of the moment of her awakening. The day she stood still as the sea raged beside her, threatening to engulf her, but instead of being afraid, she felt the pain beneath the wrath and knew it as her own. And it was in this moment that heaven knew earth, and earth knew heaven.

Lioness speaks.

You were a brave little girl, and you are a heroic woman.

You have survived the tumbling and crumbling of many homesteads, and yes, the foundation you are on now—the one you have been painting into existence—is guaranteed to never crumble.

Rest assured, your love for Nikki and hers for you shall return. It never left, you see. It was simply buried under an illusion of loss. Be patient. Be like the heron who would say to you, "Patience is not empty waiting. It is inner certainly."

Invite Nikki to join you in your sandbox of stability. Just as the limbs of trees that bend but do not break and seaweed that gets tossed with the tides but is not uprooted, so will your castle endure the test of time. Nikki is a painter too. An artist of dreams and castles. She painted the brilliant cover of your book. She took the photographs of you—all its holograms birthed from love and inner eyes that saw the soul of you, and now you see lovingly into hers. Love is never lost dear one. It is a new day. A new song is being sung with new words and new melodies.

Potentialities. Never impossibilities.

Rejoice because it is here where the once-raging lioness, the one who resided within you, is tamed, is at peace and has laid her head down with the innocence of the lamb.

Living With a Mental Illness: Opening to Grace

This entry was taken directly out of a diary and later placed in my first published book, *Re-Write Your Life: A Transformational Guide to Writing and Healing the Stories of Our Lives*.

It is now an online self-study program. You'll find the link to the program in the Resource section at the end of the book.

One day my mother sat me down and told me she didn't know what to do to make me feel better. That it felt too big for her to carry. She wanted me to go with her to the hospital, where some doctors would talk to me.

"They'll know what to do, honey," she tried to smile. "They will make you feel like Junie again. They'll bring back our Junie, I promise," she cried, wiping back tears.

I sat there horrified but couldn't speak. With that, she put me in the car and drove me to the Branson Hospital on Finch Avenue in Toronto. I was in absolute terror as they admitted me. When my mother left me that day, I thought my life was over.

"Mommy, please don't go. Please, Mommy! Don't go!" I inwardly screamed.

I was an infant trapped in a twenty-year-old body, and the only thing that mattered was that my mommy was going away, and now I would surely die.

Life on the ward was unbearable. I was expected to sit in 'the lounge' with other crazies like me and watch the world go by. Every now and then, they would call us into a larger room where we would sit on chairs in a circle and be asked to talk about how we were feeling. I had no language. I could not talk. And the people in the other chairs terrified me. I wanted my mommy. More, I wanted to die. "God strike me dead," I begged from a hollow cave inside me. I hid in my room. They'd come and get me and take me back to the lounge. I'd slip back to my room. They'd come and get me again. There was nowhere to go. I had nowhere else to hide. And nothing was helping. None of the umpteen medications they had me on nor the individual or group therapies. My mother and father came every day. So did Joseph, the man who loved me no matter what. I was told my siblings came as well, but I have no recollection of that. I just remember living for the visits from my mom and wanting to end my life every time she left.

At the end of a very long month, the doctor told my parents there was nothing else they could do for me. He said that I probably used a lot of drugs while I was away in Europe and that there's no telling if I'll ever come out of it. He went on to tell them that I may have damaged my brain cells irreparably. He said he was sorry, but they could take me home now. I knew he was lying. I never did drugs. I couldn't defend myself. There was a veil between me and them. I could hear, but I couldn't speak. But I could go home! That was all that mattered. I was never so happy in my life. I was also never so terrified. I was just condemned to a living death—to be this way forever."

Addendum: Mental Illness doesn't come out of nowhere. It's not a toxic pollutant in the air that gets inhaled other than what gets inhaled energetically in one's living environment day in and day out, and if there is a genetic propensity—well then, you may have won the lottery. That was my experience. I won it at twenty years old, and the only place to cash in with a very sick, unrelenting ruminating mind of suicidal ideation is dead or a hospital bed, or what I did. Every day, I summoned every tiny thread of courage I could find to keep putting one foot in front of the other. To go beyond someone else's label and identity for me. I prayed and looked for solutions that would bring me inner peace—and more—something to give me meaning and a reason to live.

Madness, Masks and Miracles

I wrote this play to dispel myths and stigmas about mental illness. It's about the madness or dark night of the soul that all humans go through as we walk this earth, the masks, heartbreak, fear, anger, and confusion we wear so we can pretend everything is fine and the miracles that allow us to feel safe enough to finally take off the masks and be our true, authentic, beautiful selves, just as we are.

The play was birthed out of unrelenting pain—what I call "the torture chamber of my mind."

I managed to capture a few moments of what I was experiencing on the pages of my journal during some of my worst bouts with bipolar illness.

After another hospitalization, I kept getting a strong inner message to write my story in the form of a play. I fought it for many months until I finally succumbed. I invited a professional actor, Victoria Maxwell, who had the same diagnosis, to join me in the writing. It was a collaboration fraught with everything from excitement to grief to joy and finally to a staged performance called Madness, Masks and Miracles.

The play brought out the greater truth that although mental illness can affect anyone regardless of intelligence, social class, or income level, the people living with it are frequently the victims of an ignorant society.

The play also clearly portrays that we are all innocent and loving beings under each of our masks. And it's only when we feel safe enough to shed these masks and speak authentically from our hearts that the madness ends and the miracles begin.

Here is what Dr. Michael Meyers, President of the Canadian Psychiatric Association, had to say:

"This play is a winner. June Swadron and her writing team and actors engage the audience immediately and throughout with what it's like to have a mental illness in contemporary society. We feel the anguish and confusion, we witness the denial in co-workers and family, we experience the shame of the sufferer and the multiple losses, and we learn painfully about the limitations of our treatments. Yet this production is not cynical or depressing. It is moving, inspiring and intensely evocative. A gift. A call-to-arms. A must-see for every Canadian citizen."

"Phobia Song"

Madness, Masks and Miracles had several moments of comic relief. One of them was this song, written by me and scribbled in my journal years before the play was even conceived.

Fear of dying and afraid of life
Fear of flying and afraid of strife
Fear of losing and afraid to win
Goodness Gracious! Where does one begin!

Claustrophobia, Agoraphobia, and phobias we can't spell
Pathophobia, Xenophobia, Hydrophobia, Zoophobia
We know 'em well.
Now what would Freud or Jung say
If they were in this room?
Their likely fear would be to get out of here
In case they caught the gloom!

Are we crazy, no we're not,
We're simply concerned by what we've got
Fear of hunger, afraid of fat
Fear of wars, chores, and doors
Can you imagine that!

Fear of Satan and afraid of God
Is there anything here we're not afraid of?

Between our birth and dying, we have so much to fear
Was God, do you think, in His right mind?
To ever have put us here!
Fear of cats and afraid of snakes
Fear of laughter for goodness' sake
Fear of ageing or growing too tall
Face it. If it's not worth fearing, is it worth it at all?

Afraid of getting out of bed, a fear of eternal sin
Afraid of germs, afraid of worms, afraid of your own kin!
Afraid of black, afraid of white, afraid of in-between
Afraid of going out alone, afraid of being seen

Are we crazy, well maybe yes
You decide. It's anyone's guess
Are we crazy, well maybe not
Isn't it something that everyone's got?

Goodbye Papa

The following piece is taken from notes I found in my journal
shortly after my father's death and later repurposed for my book,
*Re-Write Your Life: A Transformational Guide to Writing and
Healing the Stories of Our Lives.*

We sat there watching to see if he was still breathing. Day after
day. Sometimes we spoke; other times, we were lost in our own
worlds, unconnected in almost every way except for the blood tie
that brought us here. It had only been two or three days that he'd

been in a coma, but the doctors were talking about taking him off life support, pulling out the plug.

After the shock wore off, it seemed the reasonable, even compassionate thing to do for everyone except my mother. Dad had been slowly dying for two years. We understood her resistance, her terror of him leaving her after forty-eight years of marriage. But he had already left her. She couldn't acknowledge that. "Don't you bring those funeral faces to my door," she implored months and months ago. That was even before he was in this state but already looking feeble and gaunt, and cancer had eaten up two-thirds of his body. "Where there's life, there's hope," she declared repeatedly as if to convince herself of a truth even she could hardly believe.

But we had already started to grieve. I remember walking around with a permanent lump in my chest that just wouldn't go away. Now, here in this hospital room, we spoke lovingly before him.

Some of us were with him all day long. Howard, for instance, never left. He held his hand from morning to night. His only son. The one with whom he never saw eye to eye. Others came after work—his other children, grandchildren, sisters, and his one remaining brother.

We'd tell each other the stories of our days. Sometimes we laughed and joked. Then, as if it were wrong, we'd retreat into silence and go separate again. But our being together in this love-filled room with a dying man seemed to dissolve any of the distance we felt between us. The anger, the resentment didn't matter here. They were gone. I basked in the love because I knew that all too soon, it would end, and we would go back to our other lives and our unhealed hearts.

I don't know how much love Mom was able to let in from any of us during this time. Fear, pain, and anger seemed to fuel the pump that kept her going. She was adamant for him to live, no matter what his condition. "Where there is life, there is hope," she insisted again and again.

Gently and away from his room, we tried to dissuade her. "Think of Dad, Mom. He is in pain. He has so little fight left and is so tired. Try to let him go," was how we put it.

Ten minutes before my father took his final breath, and after thirty-six hours of an uninterrupted coma, my father opened his eyes. They were as clear as stars. They were so full of love that I have never witnessed anything more beautiful, more remarkable in my life.

Mom was sitting beside him. When she took Dad's hand this time, she tenderly spoke, "I love you, Jimmy. I love you so much. What are you trying to tell me? That you love me too? I know you do, darling. Your children are all here. I am going to be fine, sweetheart. Truly I am. You do what you must and know that our love will always be with you."

Tears fell softly from my father's eyes. He could not speak. He could not move. But the love expressed in his eyes said more than words could ever hope to do. I wasn't sure if I believed in miracles before this. No one has to convince me now.

My father awoke from his coma to say goodbye.

Living Spaces

This writing came from a writing prompt—one you will find in this book. It turned into a wonderful recounting of where I lived during my childhood and teen years. I invite you to try this writing prompt as it can act as a springboard to catapult you into writing a collection of stories from your life.

It's quite remarkable how many ways one can interpret a word. One simple word. In this case, space. How much space is there in space? Where does space start, and where does it end? Is there going to be enough space for Harold to bring everything he decided to cram into his one-bedroom apartment from his six-bedroom house? Where's he going to put it all? Where will he sit? It's not like he wasn't always a hoarder. It's just that he had more space to amass his "just in case I'll need it one day" sundry whatever's at his former address.

When I was a child, we lived in a three-bedroom apartment. There was a room for my parents, a room for me and my two sisters and one for my older brother, Howard. I shared his room until I was about eight, and then, after too many fights over who was going to shut the bedroom light off and other inane outbursts—I was relegated to a tiny cot in my sisters' room until Lorraine got married a year later. Barbara was next when I was twelve, and finally, I had my very own bedroom. Now I could claim all that space for myself. Trust me, I embraced that luxury with bravado!

The thing is, my mother was not just a neat freak. She was a neat freak, and she was a crazy-clean freak. I'm talking about all objects meticulously positioned in their perfect place—and, of course, our apartment was antiseptic clean.

In those days, everyone we knew seemed to smoke. It was the thing. Mom would be running over to put the ashtray under— even a guest's cigarette, just in time before an unsuspecting ash— God forbid—landed on the carpet.

Speaking of carpets, we had a white shag rug which she vacuumed and raked faithfully every day. Not just once. Often. I must admit, it did look lovely when it was freshly raked, every fibre of the white virgin wool standing erect complimenting the classical baby blue sofa, black and gold French Provincial coffee table graced with a crystal vase containing a dozen long stem red roses, presented to her lovingly each week by my dad.

There were adjacent ends tables upon which sat elegant gold-trimmed black lamps adorning pearl-white oval shades. I must give her this—she did take the plastic off the shades, whereas many relatives kept it on till they yellowed and then replaced the plastic.

Our living room also sported a scarlet-red French Provincial chaise lounge along with a comfy recliner chair that, when men sat on it, the change in their pockets would unsuspectedly pour out and disappear into its creases which I would happily collect when they walked away to add to my piggy bank collection.

We also had the long consul stereo and television unit circa 19050 where my mom would croon along with Dean Martin at the top of her lungs, "Love me with all of your heart, that's all I want love," or sway to Artie Shaw's big band sound. We watched *The Ed Sullivan Show* faithfully every Sunday night after Bonanza. I would turn on *Dick Clarke's American Band Stand* every day after school, and Mom and I would jive in between the furniture to Bobby Darin and Diana Ross and The Supremes.

Above the consul was a painting I adored. It was of an 18th-century Victorian parlour. One of the ladies of the manor stood on a winding staircase in her flowing royal blue gown, playing the violin while her sister sat elegantly at the baby grand piano, accompanying her to what I often imagined was Beethoven, Bach, or Rachmaninoff. I put myself into that portrait, enabling me to believe I was one of those ladies of leisure living a cultured and privileged life. It was really me sitting poised at that piano. This was in direct contrast to Dad's hardworking job as a cab driver by day and a projectionist in the movie theatres by night, all the while struggling to make ends meet.

Our small apartment was the perfect model suite except for the fact that a family of six was supposedly living there. Besides the one comfy pickpocket chair, you wouldn't want to touch anything lest it broke or moved a millimetre, sending my mom scrambling to reset, unruffle, dust or put back that which was singular, to her eyes only, now dreadfully out of place.

God help you if walked in the door without first removing your shoes. Although, even shoeless, your socks left deep colossal caverns in the perfectly coiffed white shag rug. Sometimes when we had a lot of company, it looked like a jammed highway collision with nasty footprints crisscrossing every which way. My mother could not go to sleep until she raked the carpet back to its perfect pristine posture. Me, I got used to walking backwards, rake in hand, carefully hiding my footprints so there would be no detection of my human presence. Too bad none of us learned how to fly or levitate over that darn rug. I'm guessing this insanity may have contributed to feeling invisible for much of my life. You can now guess where it originated when I speak about taking up too much space.

The weird thing in all of this is that if you didn't know how neurotic it all was and you walked into our apartment as a stranger, you would marvel at the elegance before your eyes. Oh yes, it was classy and chic, all right. As was Mom. At any time of the day, she looked like she just stepped out of Vogue Magazine. Simply an unexpected sight for an ordinary apartment building on a street that had the exact same brown, ugly buildings lining the block.

Luckily for me, once Lorraine and Barbara were gone and I had my own room, I could close the door and keep my space any way I wanted. I placed a sign on the door that said, "Disaster Area, Keep Out"—and apart from my friends, no one ever entered. It was my one place to be a rebel in an otherwise perfect setting. It kind of backfired from time to time, as there was no room in which to move. I had to crawl over the bed to get to the other side of the room. Still, I could be as sloppy and messy as I wanted, and nobody chastised me for it! I was free!

Clothes stayed wherever they landed long after they came off my body. And, well, you couldn't really see my treasures without going on a true treasure hunt—under Hudson Bay blankets and my pink knobby bedspread with magazines tossed every which way. In fact, my room consisted of a single bed with a tiny bed-side table holding my pink princess phone, a prized gift for my sixteenth birthday.

On the floor beside my bed was one of my two other prized possessions. My portable record player and a stack of 45s and LPs, which were scattered everywhere. On the other side of the bed was a chipped wooden desk with a laminated top showing a map of the world with pencil cases, schoolbooks, comic books, and Mad Magazines stacked on top of it.

But my favourite possession of all, if one can actually 'possess' a living creature, was Elvis, my precious blue budgie bird named after Elvis Presley, of course. He officially belonged to Lorraine until she got married and moved to Europe with her husband.

Elvis's cage sat by the window facing the expansive field just beyond our building. Every day when I got home from school, hearing my voice, he'd start singing and whistling or screeching, "Hurry up, get me out of here!" And I would. I'd open his cage door, flop onto my bed and he'd fly and flop onto the pillow beside me. He'd immediately start telling me all about his day a mile a minute in gibberish.

What fascinated me most was that this tiny little creature and I had an emphatic, intimate communication between us. Sometimes I would fall asleep and wake up, and he'd be sitting there on my pillow by my head, just silently looking at me. It's hard to describe. Our connection was deeper than with any human I knew at the time. Maybe ever. We were both completely safe in each other's gaze. And when he died, I was left with a big empty space in my eleven-year-old heart. Yet, ironically, as these things often go, the emptiness of a beloved's passing is replaced and filled with memories overflowing with love, making that space more sacred.

Yes, the many interpretations and transformations of spaces.

Spaces as tiny as bird cages housing birds pleading to fly free and spaces without limits—the kind my imagination would take me to and yet the thing I was criticized for the most in school. "June, stop daydreaming!" more than one teacher would shout. Or my favourite when I excitedly described something that was to me a fantastic idea, surely worth exploring—only to be greeted with, "Are you nuts? Take your head out of the clouds, girl and get real!" I didn't want to, so I escaped into more pleasurable spaces and places as often as possible. Some of my shrinks called it disassociating. I called it bliss!

On warm summer nights with the window open, I'd hear the crickets in the grass, the frogs croaking in the creek, and the fireflies crackling as they lit up the chestnut trees. Those nights when everyone else slept that untamed field with all its creatures was my escape into spaces beyond this earthly plane, and I was in heaven.

Later the Parks Department commissioned workers to come in and convert my beautiful field that carried the best of my childhood into a manicured park. But I'll always remember the long, leisurely, hot summer days lying on my back, safely camouflaged by tall grasses, while gazing at the sky mesmerized by the angels appearing as clouds. Or I'd crouch down and be ever so still and ever so quiet so as not to disturb the praying mantises right by my feet while they prayed.

That untamed field was my safe haven away from the madness that lived inside the walls of my mother's castle. But the city decided to convert my sacred space into a regular park with swings, teeter-totters, slides, a merry-go-round, and three park benches for the old folk.

But to tell the truth, the timing suited us as we were becoming teenagers then, and it was not only home to the little kids and the old folk in the neighbourhood; it became the teenage hangout.

Word spread, and it seemed like every teenager north of Lawrence Avenue could be found at the Wasdale/Neptune Park. Oh yes, there we all were, on any given evening, listening to the sounds of the Beatles, Dave Clarke Five, Dylan and Peter Paul and Mary on our little transistor radios. My, oh my, life was so sweet and innocent then.

Yet given time, everything changes. Sometimes I get nostalgic for my early years at 57 Neptune Drive. A few years ago, I met up with my best friend, Suki, who lived across the park from me. We reunited after a hiatus of forty-three years and living 3,000 miles apart. I returned home on a visit to Toronto, and we walked around the old neighbourhood and reminisced. Having a best friend who goes back to the time you were six years old, sharing all the inner and outer places and spaces we've traversed since then, was precious and sweet.

I do have to say I became more like my mother in the end. Although I started in my own dwellings that looked a lot like my bedroom did years ago, I inadvertently discovered I had a knack for interior design. Today, our house is very eclectic in its fur-nishings—nothing matches—but somehow, it all seems to work. Colours, fabrics, art, and music grace each of the rooms, and I am not ashamed to admit that my favourite pastime is rearranging the furniture.

Give me a space, and I'll create something magical. And if you can't find me, check out the garage sales. I'll be sorting through the selections of other people's throwaways to add to my own "just in case" collection. Hmm, kind of reminds me of Harold. I wonder how he made out with all those things in the end. I sure hope he found enough space to put them in.

"Where Did It Go"

The following journal entry is a fun poem that I later read aloud in an open mike, Spoken Word evening. It's about an idea that popped into my head, and instead of writing it down, I got distracted and did other things. Of course, by the time I decided to put pen to paper, my idea was completely gone. Well, rather than sulk, I wrote a rant instead. Word to the wise—if you suddenly get an epiphany or a light-bulb moment, as my friend, Tom Evans, loves to call it, capture it in the moment. Don't wait!

"Where Did It Go"

It was just a moment ago
I composed a poem in my head
And came as quickly as I could
To grab my pen and catch the thread
But none comes back. It's a brutal attack
Upon my more...sophisticated...self-image.

Image that. A brilliant poem
Travelling through my mind
And no matter how I muse and wonder
Fret, focus, or growl with thunder
Not a sentence, a phrase, a word that stays
No, it's all gone asunder.

So, what to do now stuck with you
A page of untouched blankness
Cold, bleak, startlingly weak
You ask me to feed you frankness!

Fine, I say. But don't ask for rhyme
There isn't the time
And don't expect wit or humour
It was all there before
Brilliant, magic, and much, much more.
But where did it go? I don't know
And I can't get it back
It's that amnesia attack
That's come to steal my show!

Sneaky, covert, sly, and alert
It deserves awards
For its cunning acts of shame
So, am I the one who must be shunned?
Who loses her fun, a day in the sun?
When it's the menace to blame!

Oh yes, it's a pity.
I created this whole ditty
And now cannot recite it.
Believe me, I say, it was a brilliant bouquet
But how can I even fight it?

But it's not my fault. No, no, not at all
The fact that I cannot recall
Amnesia is an untreatable ill

It has its own indestructible will
So why do I go on fumbling still just to please you?
Okay! Okay! Yes, blank page
You need to be fed
Well, consider this your meal for the day I've had my fill.
I'm taking to bed
I'm not a robot. I'm a poet instead
I have dignity, you know
Consider this your show
And besides, I need my rest
To save up for the best
So, I bid you adieu.
Good Day!

Part Seven
WRITE WHERE YOU ARE—FINALLY!

I could have summed up the whole book under this one heading. Here's why writing from where you are works; writing from where you are allows you to stay in the present time. It's about the here and now and honouring that. Even if you are writing about your seventh birthday, remembering running down the stairs to see what your mom and dad bought you, the excitement you feel in your body, even though it was over forty years ago, brings it back as though it was happening right now and that's what's relevant.

There is a Buddhist saying that when you eat, you simply eat; when you walk, you simply walk; and today, when you write, you simply write. When you do this, you build a foundation for your writing. A foundation that you can covet because it is yours alone. And, when you access your truth from the place of which I speak, paradoxically, your voice is universal. You tap into the voice of humanity. Because underneath the layers of our external lives and the masks we sometimes wear, we all breathe the same heart song.

And simply put, this heart song is to love and be loved, to be at peace, and to be joyous. Writing reveals this. You know it every time you hear a poem or read a novel or listen to the words of a song that moves you deeply. You also know that whoever penned that inspired work has reached into their belly and touched their soul and reached the humanity within us all.

Writing from where you are is a journey into self-discovery, which can involve confronting the parts of yourself that have been hidden or repressed. This is where your energy and passion are. It's the authentic you. It's original thought.

Don't be afraid to go right to the marrow. There may be things that scare you. That's okay; keep writing. Eventually, you will get to the other side and feel better. This brings healing, catharsis, and clarity. At other times, you will feel spent. What you are doing is powerful. You are letting your energy flow through you instead of letting it get buried or stuck or playing pretend with poetic words or half-truths that sound nice but don't describe what is truly going on.

Write through your feelings, not around them.

Honouring yourself with your truth is what liberates you. And hopefully, I have described that well in the preceding pages. However, you won't know that until you put down this book, pick up your journal, and write where you are.

Part Eight

A Brand-New Blank Page- Go Crazy, Go Sane, Just Write Where You Are!

This is a special place for you to draw or colour, create mind maps, write poetry, or take off in any direction. Oh, and be sure to write everything you love about this book and write-fully so! Mostly, have fun!

I hope you have enjoyed the read as much as I have enjoyed writing it.

May your journal become a true friend to you—a sacred place where you can rest your head on the page with your words or take off into the land of creative explosion!

Above all, always remember that Ray Bradbury not only says to write every day, but he also recommends staying drunk on writing so that your reality can't destroy you. So, stay creative, stay connected and always write where you are.

Love and blessings,

Junie

_____

_____

_____

_____

_____

_____

_____

_____

_____

_____

_____

_____

_____

_____

_____

_____

_____

_____

_____

_____

_____

_____

_____

_____

_____

About the Author
BY THE AUTHOR, MOI!

In my inimitable fashion—not short—it's a story. Go grab a cuppa tea.

So, you really want to know more about me and why I've been facilitating sacred writing circles for over three decades when getting a steady job would have been far more lucrative? Okay, here goes:

Possibly because I'm bipolar and don't always make rational decisions! However, more in keeping with the truth, it's because I am passionate about writing and want to share my excitement with people who want to write as well. And I couldn't have continued year after year if I didn't see rewarding results time and time again.

As written in Part Seven, "From Journals to Jewels," one of the biggest turning points of my life came because of writing my play that exposed the fact that I have bipolar illness and the terror I felt about being judged. I fought my way through the pages of many journals until I finally surrendered to the bigger truth that my story needed to be told—not just because of what it could do for me but for countless others who suffer from the same illness.

Madness, Masks, and Miracles depicts the madness or the dark night of the soul, I believe we all face while trying to find our way in life, the masks we wear to hide the madness, pain, shame, fear, heartbreak, and the miracles that allow us to take off our masks and be real.

Years later, I penned and published, *Re-Write Your Life: A Transformational Guide to Writing and Healing the Stories of Our Lives*, so others could experience liberation through a conscious writing process.

Imagine if they gave hospital patients a steady supply of journals to do the same. And imagine if one of the mandates of the caregivers was to sit and have a conversation with each patient—perhaps even listening to what they wrote, paying full attention to their needs, and offering understanding and compassion. "Oh my," as Louis Armstrong so beautifully sang out, "What a wonderful world this could be."

Some people have accused me of living my life with rose-coloured glasses, not seeing reality as it is. When I would succumb to those comments because it was too hard to be me, I would let my spirit die. Luckily, my journal would rescue me and bring me back to life. I would then equip those people with pen and paper and coerce them to follow my lead. I now have a back-end business selling rose-coloured glasses, pens, and paper—and making a fortune—and writing books like this one!

Shall I take your order now?

Resources
EVIDENCE-BASED POWER OF JOURNALING FOR ALL YOU DISBELIEVERS!

If you've come this far, I'm counting on the fact that you are a convert by now and well into your first number-one bestseller. Below you'll find a list of resources which attest to the power of journaling as a healing modality. For the past decade, an increasing number of studies have demonstrated that when individuals write about emotional experiences, significant physical and mental health improvements follow.

Writing about Emotional Experiences as a Therapeutic Process by James W. Pennebaker

The Power of Journaling: Can Journaling Help Us Cope During Troubled Times? by David B. Feldman Ph.D.

The Power of Journaling by Brian A. Klems

What's All This About Journaling? by Hayley Phelan

Expressive Writing in Psychological Science by James W. Pennebaker

Counting Blessings Versus Burdens: An Experimental Investigation of Gratitude and Subjective Well-being in Daily Life. National Library of Medicine by Robert A Emmons 1, Michael E McCullough

Other Books by the Author

For information about Junie's workshops, online programmes, and retreats, go to:

http://junieswadron.com.
https://junieswadron.com/re-write-your-life-self-paced/

And please join me on my weekly Sunday Sacred Writing Circles and my Junie's Writing Sanctuary on Facebook.

https://www.facebook.com/groups/387478408118428

Other books by the author:
https://junieswadron.com/junies-publications/

Your Life Matters: 8 Simple Steps to Writing Your Story
"For those with a burning desire to write their memoir, Junie torches every negative emotion, cuts through the harsh inner critic who sets up our self-imposed obstacles and illuminates the pathway to liberation. Junie sets the stage for the freedom to reveal the life stories that will make a fabulously interesting journey of self-discovery for the writer as well as the reader. Brilliant!"
Judith Rockert

Re-Write Your Life: A Transformational Guide to Writing and Healing the Stories of Our Lives

"Junie Swadron is both a guide and a muse. Her book is a bright lantern, illuminating the often dark and tricky terrain of the soul. Grounded in personal experience, her techniques catalyze the deep authenticity possible to us all."

Julia Cameron, author of *The Artist's Way*.

Madness, Masks and Miracles: A Play to Dispel Myths and Stigmas about Mental Illness

co-written by Junie Swadron & Victoria Maxwell

"This play is a winner. June Swadron and her writing team and actors engage the audience immediately and throughout with what it's like to have a mental illness in contemporary society. We feel the anguish and confusion, we witness the denial in co-workers and family, we experience the shame of the sufferer and the multiple losses, and we learn painfully about the limitations of our treatments. Yet this production is not cynical or depressing. It is moving, inspiring, and intensely evocative. A gift. A call-to-arms. A must-see for every Canadian citizen."

Dr. Michael Meyers, President of the Canadian Psychiatric Association

Colouring Your Dreams Come True: A Bedtime Story and Colouring Book for Children of All Ages and the Child within Every Adult

Jazzy's Miracle Mission: A True Story Colouring Book

A free ebook edition is available with the purchase of this book.

To claim your free ebook edition:

1. Visit MorganJamesBOGO.com
2. Sign your name CLEARLY in the space
3. Complete the form and submit a photo of the entire copyright page
4. You or your friend can download the ebook to your preferred device

Morgan James BOGO™

A **FREE** ebook edition is available for you or a friend with the purchase of this print book.

CLEARLY SIGN YOUR NAME ABOVE

Instructions to claim your free ebook edition:
1. Visit MorganJamesBOGO.com
2. Sign your name CLEARLY in the space above
3. Complete the form and submit a photo of this entire page
4. You or your friend can download the ebook to your preferred device

Print & Digital Together Forever.

Snap a photo   Free ebook   Read anywhere